Grammar

Form and Function 3A

Second Edition

WORKBOOK

Milada Broukal
Amy Parker

Mc Graw Hill

Grammar Form and Function, 2nd Edition 3A Workbook

English Adaptation 2011

Published by McGraw-Hill ESL/ELT, a business unit of The McGraw-Hill Companies, Inc., 1221 Avenue of the Americas, New York, NY 10020.

Original ISBN: 978-0-07-310411-9

Editorial director: Tina B. Carver
Executive editor: Erik Gundersen
Senior developmental editor: Annie Sullivan
Editorial assistant: Kasey Williamson
Production manager: MaryRose Malley
Cover design: Preface, Inc.
Interior design: Preface, Inc.

Photo credits:
All photos are courtesy of Getty Images Royalty-Free Collection.

0 1 2 3 4 5 6 7 8 9 20 Artec 2024

When ordering this title, please use

ISBN 10: 89-6055-201-1
ISBN 13: 978-89-6055-201-2

Printed in Korea

Contents

UNIT 1 THE PRESENT

UNIT 2 THE PAST

UNIT 3 THE FUTURE

UNIT 4 NOUNS AND EXPRESSIONS OF QUANTITY

UNIT 5 PRONOUNS AND ARTICLES

UNIT 6 MODALS I

UNIT 7 MODALS II

UNIT 1 THE PRESENT

1a The Simple Present and The Present Progressive

Student Book p. 2

1 Practice

Complete the sentences with the simple present or the present progressive of the verbs in parentheses. If there are other words in the parentheses, include them.

Jenna: Hi, Mark! I (never, see) ____________ (1) you outside this early in the morning. Where (you, go) ____________ (2)?

Mark: I (run) ____________ (3) to the park right now. These days I (try) ____________ (4) to work out every morning before work. I (want) ____________ (5) to lose weight. My doctor said that exercise (be) ____________ (6) the most important thing you can do. What about you? Why (be) ____________ (7) you up so early?

Jenna: I (work out) ____________ (8) this morning, too. I usually (get up) ____________ (9) at six to work out.

Mark: That's great. What (you, do) ____________ (10) to stay in shape?

Jenna: Sometimes I (jog) ____________ (11) around the neighborhood. I often (take) ____________ (12) a yoga class at the gym. But unfortunately, it (become) ____________ (13) more difficult to find the time and energy to exercise.

Mark: Oh, really? Why (be) ____________ (14) it so hard? (be) ____________ (15) you busy with work?

Jenna: Yes, I (be) ______ (16). Sometimes I (come) ______ (17) home late, and often I (stay) ______ (18) up late finishing work. It (get) ______ (19) harder to wake up early.

Mark: It (be) ______ (20) hard for me to get up in the morning and exercise, too. But I (not, be) ______ (21) busy with work. I just (not, like) ______ (22) to exercise!

2 Practice

Complete the questions and answers with the simple present or the present progressive of the verbs in parentheses. If there are other words in the parentheses, include them.

Doctor: How (you, feel) ______ (1) these days, Rob?

Rob: I (not, do) ______ (2) very well at the moment. I hurt my knee last Sunday, and the pain (get) ______ (3) worse. My knee (constantly, hurt) ______ (4).

Doctor: (you, take) ______ (5) any medication right now?

Rob: No, I (not, take) ______ (6) anything at the moment.

Doctor: (you, exercise) ______ (7) regularly?

Rob: No, I don't. I (not, have, usually) ______ (8) time. Although I (play, sometimes) ______ (9) basketball with my friends on weekends.

Doctor: Which knee (bother) ______ (10) you?

Rob: My right knee.

Doctor: (it, hurt) ______ (11) when you bend your knee?

Rob: No, it (not, do) ______________ (12). But I (feel, always) ______________ (13) pain when I straighten it.

Doctor: How (your knee, feel) ______________ (14) when I move it this way?

Rob: Ouch!

Doctor: You needed to see a doctor as soon as this happened. Who (be) ______________ (15) your regular doctor?

Rob: I (see, usually) ______________ (16) Dr. Berman. But he (be) ______________ (17) on vacation this week.

3 Practice

Match the sentences with the uses of the simple present and the present progressive.

Simple Present Tense	Present Progressive Tense
a. permanent situation	d. action in progress
b. repeated action	e. changing situation
c. general truth	f. action in progress around the present

_____ **1.** Susan works as a programmer at a computer company in Seattle.

_____ **2.** Many people in the computer industry are losing their jobs these days.

_____ **3.** There used to be many programming jobs in Seattle, but it is getting more difficult to find a job in today's economy.

_____ **4.** Many companies advertise jobs in the newspaper.

_____ **5.** Susan reads the job ads every morning.

_____ **6.** A company called "Software Solutions" is hiring computer programmers right now!

4 Practice

Read the sentences. Write *C* next to the sentence if the simple present or the present progressive is used correctly. Write *I* if it is used incorrectly.

_____ **1.** Why you studying English at this school?

_____ **2.** Public transportation becomes more important in our crowded city.

_____ **3.** My sister is constantly borrowing my clothes.

_____ **4.** Because of her new diet, she's not eat bread now.

_____ **5.** These days, I'm working part time and going to school.

_____ **6.** Which movie you want to see?

_____ **7.** In the evenings, we like to walk around the neighborhood.

_____ **8.** Where do you working at present?

5 Practice

Look at the photo. Write four sentences using the simple present and four sentences using the present progressive. Try to include some negatives and questions.

Simple Present

1. ______________________________

____

2. ______________________________

____

3. ______________________________

____

4. ______________________________

Present Progressive

5. ______________________________

6. ______________________________

7. ______________________________

8. ______________________________

1b Nonaction (Stative) and Action Verbs

Student Book p. 7

6 Practice

Complete the sentences with the simple present or the present progressive of the verbs in parentheses. If there are negative words in the parentheses, include them.

27 **January 10, 2005**

Restaurant Review: The Boston Bistro

If you (look) ________________ (1) for excellent food and a pleasant dining experience, do not eat at the Boston Bistro. First of all, the food (be) ________________ (2) terrible. The meat (be) ________________ (3) tough and overcooked; it (require) ________________ (4) a very sharp knife to cut it. I (love) ________________ (5) garlic, but the pasta sauce (smell) ________________ (6) too strongly of garlic. Strangely, the sauce (not, taste) ________________ (7) like garlic — it (seem) ________________ (8) to have no flavor at all! Finally, the menu (not, have) ________________ (9) many choices.

The food (not, be) ________________ (10) the only bad part of the Boston Bistro. The dining room (appear) ________________ (11) crowded because there are so many tables pushed together. Personally, I usually (not, enjoy) ________________ (12) the sound of loud conversations around me while I (try) ________________ (13) to enjoy a quiet meal. Also, the servers always (seem) ________________ (14) too busy to pay attention to you.

Above all, the food (cost) ________________ (15) too much. I (realize) ________________ (16) many nice restaurants (charge) ________________ (17) more than $25.00 for dinner these days. But for $28.00, I (prefer) ________________ (18) to have excellent food and excellent service. I (fear) ________________ (19) that at those high prices, the Boston Bistro won't be in business for long.

7 Practice

Decide if each sentence has a stative or an active meaning. Then complete the sentences with the correct form of the verbs in parentheses.

1. (think)

He ________________ about quitting his job. However, he __________ ________________ it might be a bad idea.

2. (taste)

She __________ the ice cream cone right now. It ______________ like a coconut.

3. (smell)

The refrigerator ____________________ terrible. She __________ ____________________ the refrigerator after returning from her vacation.

4. (appear)

The woman ________________ very tired. She ______________________ in a play every night this week.

5. (be)

She __________________ very quiet. She __________________ quiet because she is working in a library.

1c The Present Perfect and The Present Perfect Progressive

Student Book p. 12

8 Practice

Complete the sentences with the present perfect or the present perfect progressive of the verbs in parentheses. Sometimes both tenses are possible. If both are possible, use the present perfect progressive.

A. Rachel, Eric, and Denise (graduate, just) ______(1)______! They (attend) ______(2)______ this school for the past four years. All three of them (wait) ______(3)______ a long time for this special day. Rachel (study) ______(4)______ music, and she plans to continue her musical studies in the future. Eric (find, already) ______(5)______ a good job in a bank. Denise (decide) ______(6)______ to travel — she (not, go) ______(7)______ anywhere since she started school. They (not, say) ______(8)______ goodbye to all of their friends yet, and they (still, not, remove) ______(9)______ their graduation caps and gowns. They (be) ______(10)______ too busy celebrating their success.

B. Adina (try) ________________ to improve her grades in math for months. So far, her grades (improve) ________________.
1 2

Her teacher, Mr. Williams, (help) ________________ her. She (study) ________________ math for two hours every night. She (review) ________________ all the chapters in her math book. Adina (never, be) ________________ very good at math. She (not, earn) ________________ an "A" in math since she was in the ninth grade. She (always, prefer) ________________ English and foreign languages. But she (just, receive) ________________ an "A" on her math test.
3 4 5 6 7 8 9

9 Practice

Circle the adverbs and time expressions. Then complete the sentences with the simple past, present perfect, or present perfect progressive of the verbs in parentheses. If either the present perfect or present perfect progressive is possible, use the present perfect progressive.

A. Robin: ________________ (you, borrow) my new dress last night?
1

Joanna: No, I (not, do) ________________. I (not, borrow) ________________ your clothes in a long time. Ever since I gained a few pounds, I (not, be able to) ________________ fit into your clothes.
2 3 4

Robin: That's strange. I (think) ________________ I put the dress in my closet right after I (come) ________________ home yesterday.
5 6

B. Erica: I like your new car! When (you, buy) ______________ (1) it?

David: I (buy) ______________ (2) it at 2:00 today. I (only, have) ______________ (3) it for a few hours!

Erica: It's really bright. I (never, see) ______________ (4) you in such a colorful car. (you, own, ever) ______________ (5) a red car before?

David: No, this is my first. I (always, prefer) ______________ (6) black cars. I (drive) ______________ (7) a black car since the day I (get) ______________ (8) my driver's license.

Erica: So why (you, decide) ______________ (9) to buy a red car?

David: This one (be) ______________ (10) on sale!

C. Samantha: (you, watch) ______________ (1) the baseball game last night?

Ron: No, I (do, not) ______________ (2). I (never, like) ______________ (3) baseball.

Samantha: You're kidding! Baseball (be) ______________ (4) this country's most popular sport for almost 100 years! Everybody likes baseball!

Ron: Not me. I prefer soccer. I (be) ______________ (5) a soccer fan since I was a kid. And I (play) ______________ (6) the game for about ten years. (you, ever, see) ______________ (7) the World Cup on TV? Now that's exciting to watch.

Samantha: I (watch) ______________ (8) the World Cup two years ago. You're right; it (be) ______________ (9) exciting to watch. I think Americans (grow) ______________ (10) more interested in soccer in recent years. But I still like baseball better.

10 Practice

Circle the correct adverb and put it in the correct position. Only one adverb is correct. Rewrite each sentence with the adverb in the correct place.

1. Gina has walked to work in her new shoes. (still / just / ever)

____

____

2. She has worn such uncomfortable shoes. (ever / yet / never)

____

____

3. It is only 9:00 in the morning, but her feet have started to hurt. (yet / still / already)

____

____

4. She hasn't arrived at work. (already / yet / just)

____

11 Practice

Rewrite each sentence in Practice 10 as a question. Use the present perfect or present perfect progressive. Change adverbs if necessary.

1. ______________________________________?
2. ______________________________________?
3. ______________________________________?
4. ______________________________________?

12 Practice

Read the sentences. Write *C* next to the sentence if the present perfect or the present perfect progressive is used correctly. Write *I* if it is used incorrectly.

_____ 1. She's been having that coat for a week.

_____ 2. I so far have traveled to five countries and thirty states.

_____ 3. The students have been waiting for the teacher since 20 minutes.

_____ 4. Have they already paid for their tickets?

_____ **5.** Where has the time gone?

_____ **6.** Have ever you been to Africa?

_____ **7.** He hasn't returned the homework already.

_____ **8.** Women have been earned more money for the last ten years.

_____ **9.** How many times have you been taking the TOEFL?

_____ **10.** We've never been to that restaurant.

13 Practice

Write five statements and two questions about the people in the photo. Use the tenses given in parentheses and time expressions, adverbs, or negatives when possible.

1. (present perfect)

____

2. (present perfect progressive)

____

3. (simple past)

____

4. (simple present)

____

5. (present progressive)

____

6. (Question: present perfect)

____

7. (Question: present perfect progressive)

____

SELF-TEST

A Choose the best answer, A, B, C, or D, to complete the sentence. Mark your answer by darkening the oval with the same letter.

1. Who ____________ to join us for lunch?

A. does want Ⓐ Ⓑ Ⓒ Ⓓ
B. is wanting
C. wants
D. wanting

2. Many students ____________ at part-time jobs these days.

A. have worked Ⓐ Ⓑ Ⓒ Ⓓ
B. are working
C. working
D. are being working

3. Basketball players ____________ usually tall.

A. are being Ⓐ Ⓑ Ⓒ Ⓓ
B. are
C. have been
D. being

4. What grade ____________ in that class?

A. are you having Ⓐ Ⓑ Ⓒ Ⓓ
B. you have
C. have
D. do you have

5. Fresh coffee ____________ good in the morning.

A. is smelling Ⓐ Ⓑ Ⓒ Ⓓ
B. has been smelling
C. smells
D. smelling

6. Anne: Are you enjoying that book?
Ron: Yes, ____________.

A. I'm Ⓐ Ⓑ Ⓒ Ⓓ
B. I have
C. I am
D. I do

7. Right now, she ____________ about her vacation.

A. thinks Ⓐ Ⓑ Ⓒ Ⓓ
B. has thought
C. has been thinking
D. is thinking

8. The class ____________ $100 for their trip.

A. earns Ⓐ Ⓑ Ⓒ Ⓓ
B. has earned
C. has been earning
D. earning

9. She ____________ to borrow her parents' car.

A. is constantly asking Ⓐ Ⓑ Ⓒ Ⓓ
B. constantly asking
C. asking constantly
D. is constantly asks

10. Why ____________ TV for four hours?

A. they have watched Ⓐ Ⓑ Ⓒ Ⓓ
B. have they watched
C. have they been watching
D. they are watching

B Find the underlined word or phrase, A, B, C, or D, that is incorrect. Mark your answer by darkening the oval with the same letter.

1. He hasn't (A) answered (B) so far (C) our question about the test (D).

   Ⓐ Ⓑ Ⓒ Ⓓ

2. Mary hasn't (A) been (B) work (C) at her new job (D) for very long.

   Ⓐ Ⓑ Ⓒ Ⓓ

3. Where (A) the baseball team has (B) been (C) practicing (D) during the winter?

   Ⓐ Ⓑ Ⓒ Ⓓ

4. Have you (A) yet (B) signed up (C) for the class (D)?

   Ⓐ Ⓑ Ⓒ Ⓓ

5. Her (A) mother has been (B) waiting (C) for her for 3:00 (D) in the afternoon.

   Ⓐ Ⓑ Ⓒ Ⓓ

6. The workers are (A) painting (B) the fence since (C) early this morning (D).

   Ⓐ Ⓑ Ⓒ Ⓓ

7. I haven't (A) been (B) still (C) to any countries (D) in Asia.

   Ⓐ Ⓑ Ⓒ Ⓓ

8. What is the most exciting (A) thing you have (B) ever (C) do (D)?

   Ⓐ Ⓑ Ⓒ Ⓓ

9. Is (A) the president appears (B) on any TV shows (C) this week (D)?

   Ⓐ Ⓑ Ⓒ Ⓓ

10. Some (A) older people are believing (B) that teenagers are becoming (C) more polite (D) these days.

    Ⓐ Ⓑ Ⓒ Ⓓ

UNIT 2 THE PAST

2a The Simple Past and The Past Progressive

Student Book p. 30

1 Practice

Complete the sentences with the simple past or the past progressive of the verbs in parentheses. If there are other words in the parentheses, include them.

Police Beat: A List of Last Week's Neighborhood Crimes

A. On Saturday, April 12, a 70-year-old woman (report) ____________ (1) that her purse was stolen at Bradshaw's Supermarket. She (wait) ____________ (2) in the checkout line when she suddenly (realize) ____________ (3) she needed to buy milk. When she (leave) ____________ (4) her grocery cart to get the milk, she (forget) ____________ (5) to take her purse with her. When she (return) ____________ (6) to the cart, her purse (be) ____________ (7) gone. There (be) ____________ (8) two other people in line, two men in their 30s. The woman (ask) ____________ (9) them about her purse. They (not, see) ____________ (10) anything happen while they (stand) ____________ (11) in line. They (say) ____________ (12) that maybe she had left her purse somewhere else.

B. At 7:00 P.M. on Thursday, April 10, a man on Maple Street (water) ____________ (1) his yard when he (hear) ____________ (2) a woman screaming. He immediately (call) ____________ (3) the police on his cell phone. Then he (drop) ____________ (4) the hose and (run) ____________ (5) in the direction of the screams. At the end of the block, he (see) ____________ (6) a tall man in a blue jacket trying to take the woman's briefcase. When the tall man (notice) ____________ (7) the neighbor, he (stop) ____________ (8) what he (do) ____________ (9), (let) ____________ (10) go of the briefcase, and (turn) ____________ (11) to leave. At first he (not, seem) ____________ (12) worried about the neighbor, but then he suddenly (start) ____________ (13) to run. The neighbor (not, want) ____________ (14) the man to escape before the police (come) ____________ (15). He (yell) ____________ (16) at the tall man to stop. While the man (escape) ______________17, he (trip) ______________18 over his shoelace and (fall) ______________19 to the ground. Seconds later, while he (try) ______________20 to stand up, police (arrive) ______________21 on the scene and (arrest) ______________22 the man.

2 Practice

Complete the sentences with the simple past or the past progressive of the verbs in parentheses. If there are other words in the parentheses, include them.

Mike Willis's life has always included bicycles. Even as a very small child, he (love) ______________1 bicycles. His parents (give) ______________2 him a bike when he (be) ______________3 only four years old. In high school, he (compete) ______________4 in many races, and he (win) ______________5 a lot of money.

One day, while he (train) ______________6 for a big race, he (feel) ______________7 a sharp pain in his chest. He (ignore) ______________8 it and kept riding. But as days (pass) ______________9, the pain (not, go) ______________10 away. And it (get) ______________11 harder for him to ride his bike up hills or long distances.

Mike's parents (be) ______________12 very worried about their son. They (think) ______________13 he had a virus. They (take) ______________14 him to the doctor. The doctor (do) ______________15 many tests on Mike's blood.

The next day, while Mike (fix) ______________16 the gears on his bicycle, the doctor (call) ______________17. He (ask) ______________18 Mike to come to his office. There, the doctor (say) ______________19 that he (have) ______________20 a rare and very dangerous form of cancer. That same day, Mike (decide) ______________21 to do all he could to fight this disease. And he (promise) ______________22 himself that if he (get) ______________23 well, he would help other people with cancer.

Mike (keep) ________ (24) his promise. Six months after he (recover) ________ (25) from cancer, he (begin) ________ (26) riding his bike. Eight months later, he (go) ________ (27) on long rides again. In 2001, he (start) ________ (28) an annual bike riding event to raise money for cancer research. Three years later, more than 500 cyclists (participate) ________ (29) in this event. In 2004, the event (raise) ________ (30) nearly one million dollars for cancer research.

3 Practice

Use the prompts to write yes/no questions and answers about Mike Willis. Use the simple past or the past progressive.

1. Mike / love / bicycles / as a child

Question: ____________________?

Answer: ____________________.

2. he / win / a lot of money / from bicycle races

Question: ____________________?

Answer: ____________________.

3. Mike / see / a doctor / as soon as he felt pain

Question: ____________________?

Answer: ____________________.

4. Mike's parents / worried / about him

Question: ____________________?

Answer: ____________________.

5. Mike / ride / his bike / while he was sick

Question: ____________________?

Answer: ____________________.

6. Mike / ride / his bike / by 2001

Question: ____________________?

Answer: ____________________.

4 Practice

Use the question words to write questions about Mike Willis for the answers that follow.

1. Question: When ____?

Answer: Mike's parents gave him a bicycle when he was four years old.

2. Question: When ____?

Answer: He first felt a pain in his chest while he was training for a big race.

3. Question: What ____?

Answer: They thought he had a virus.

4. Question: What ____?

Answer: Mike was fixing the gears on his bike when the doctor called.

5. Question: How soon after his recovery ______________________________?

Answer: Mike was going on long bike rides eight months after his recovery.

6. Question: How much ____?

Answer: Mike's event raised nearly one million dollars in 2004.

7. Question: Why ____?

Answer: Mike started this event because he promised to help people fight cancer.

5 Practice

Read the sentences. What does each sentence mean? Circle *a* or *b*.

1. My sister was very happy when she learned she got the job.

a. First she was happy, and then she learned she got the job.

b. She learned she got the job, and then she was very happy.

2. My sister was wondering if she should go back to school when she learned she got the job.

a. First she was wondering if she should go back to school, and then she learned she got the job.

b. She learned she got the job, and then she wondered if she should go back to school.

3. Our parents cried when they heard the good news.

a. First our parents heard the good news, and then they cried.

b. Our parents were crying, and then they heard the good news.

4. While Jack was traveling in Europe, his dog died.

   a. First Jack's dog died, and then Jack traveled in Europe.

   b. Jack went to Europe, and then his dog died.

5. Rosa called her sister when she heard that the baby was born.

   a. First Rosa heard that the baby was born, and then she called her sister.

   b. Rosa called her sister, and then the baby was born.

6. Tom's girlfriend came over while he was taking a nap.

   a. First Tom started to take a nap, and then his girlfriend came over.

   b. Tom's girlfriend came over, and then Tom took a nap.

6 Practice

Combine the sentences into one using *while* or *when*. Use correct punctuation.

1. I studied for the final exam. I didn't want to hear the TV or the phone.

   While ______________________________.

2. I worked at two jobs. I never had any free time.

   ______________ while ______________.

3. My friends were upset. They heard we were moving to another city.

   When ______________________________.

4. Elizabeth turned 16. More than 100 guests came to her birthday party.

   ______________ when ______________.

5. Josh applied to colleges. His parents hoped he would stay close to home.

   While ______________________________.

7 Practice

Rewrite the sentences in Practice 6 with the *when* and *while* clauses in reverse order. Use correct punctuation.

1. ______________________________.
2. ______________________________.
3. ______________________________.
4. ______________________________.
5. ______________________________.

8 Practice

Complete the sentences with information about you, your friends, or your family.

1. ______________________ felt really embarrassed when ______________________

____.

2. ______________________ was very afraid when ______________________

____.

3. When ____,

______________________ was very sad.

4. When ____,

______________________ was extremely happy.

9 Practice

Choose one of the sentences you wrote in Practice 8. Use it as the first sentence of a paragraph. In at least six sentences, give more information about what happened. Use the simple past and the past progressive tenses as you tell the story.

____

____

____

____

____

____

____

____

____

____

2b The Past Perfect and The Past Perfect Progressive

Student Book p. 36

10 Practice

Complete the sentences with the simple past or the past perfect of the verbs in parentheses. If there are other words in the parentheses, include them.

Have you ever won any money? My friend Jason (feel) ______________ (1) like he did yesterday. After work, he (go) ______________ (2) to the bank to get some money. He (want) ______________ (3) to take his girlfriend Lisa out to dinner at a nice restaurant. They (not, eat) ______________ (4) at a nice restaurant for weeks. Since he (just, be) ______________ (5) paid at work, he (think) ______________ (6) it would be fun to spend a little more money.

At the cash machine, he (ask) ______________ (7) for $100.00. He (be) ______________ (8) very surprised when a large number of $20.00 bills (start) ______________ (9) flying out! He (never, see) ______________ (10) so much cash at one time. He (be) ______________ (11) alone at the machine, and he (not, know) ______________ (12) what to do. He (wonder) ______________ (13) if this (happen, ever) ______________ (14) to anyone else.

Finally, the money (stop) ______________ (15) coming out. Jason (take) ______________ (16) the $20 bills from the ground and (count) ______________ (17) them. He (could not, believe) ______________ (18) his luck. Just a few minutes earlier, he (think) ______________ (19) about taking his girlfriend somewhere nice. Now he could take her to the nicest place in town!

He (put) ______ (20) the money in his wallet. He (walk) ______ (21) away from the machine. Then he (wonder) ______ (22) if he (do) ______ (23) the right thing. Maybe the machine (be) ______ (24) broken. If so, the money (not, be) ______ (25) his to keep. Jason (bring) ______ (26) the money into the bank and (tell) ______ (27) the manager what (happen) ______ (28) to him at the cash machine. The manager said she (never, hear) ______ (29) of that happening before. She (be) ______ (30) very glad that Jason (return) ______ (31) the money.

Jason (take) ______ (32) Lisa out to dinner later that night, for less than $100. Lisa (be) ______ (33) happy. She (say) ______ (34) it was the nicest evening she (enjoy) ______ (35) in a long time. Then she said that Jason (spend) ______ (36) too much money.

II Practice

Someone took this photo of Alyssa yesterday. Why did she look so happy? Complete the sentences using the prompts and the past perfect or the past perfect progressive.

1. (get a new job)

She looked happy because

______.

2. (buy some new clothes)

She looked happy because

______.

3. (work out during her lunch hour)

She looked happy because ______.

4. (not / listen to the bad news on TV)

   She looked happy because ______________________________.

5. *(your idea)*

   She looked happy because ______________________________.

6. *(your idea)*

   She looked happy because ______________________________.

12 Practice

A journalist is interviewing an actor about his new movie. Use the prompts to write questions for the actor's answers. Write the questions in the simple past, the past perfect, or the past perfect progressive.

1. Question: When ______________________________?

   Answer: I made this movie last summer.

2. Question: ______________________________?

   Answer: No, I had never been in an action movie before.

3. Question: What kinds of movies ______________________________?

   Answer: I had acted in romances and comedies.

4. Question: Why ______________________________?

   Answer: I'd never done action movies because I wasn't in very good shape.

5. Question: Where ______________________________?

   Answer: They filmed this movie in Turkey and in France.

6. Question: ______________________________?

   Answer: No, I hadn't visited either of those countries before.

7. Question: What ______________________________?

   Answer: Before I made this movie, I'd been taking a break from acting.

8. Question: Where ______________________________?

   Answer: I'd been living in Los Angeles before I moved to New York.

9. Question: How long ____?

   Answer: I'd been working in L.A. for about five years.

10. Question: How many ____?

   Answer: I'd starred in eight movies.

13 Practice

Write six sentences about what you had or hadn't done (or been doing) by the time you sat down to do this exercise. Write three sentences using the past perfect and three sentences using the past perfect progressive. Use some negatives.

1. ____.
2. ____.
3. ____.
4. ____.
5. ____.
6. ____.

14 Practice

Complete the sentences with the present perfect progressive or the past perfect progressive of the verbs in parentheses.

1. The Larsen family is moving today. They (pack) ____________________ boxes since 6:00 in the morning.
2. Yesterday, they (pack) ____________________ for ten hours before they finally went to bed.
3. They're excited because they (want) ____________________ a bigger home for years.
4. Before they found this new home, they (complain) ____________________ that their apartment was too small for three people and two dogs.
5. They (move) ____________________ the furniture around, but it hadn't worked.
6. The Larsens were happy to find this new house because they (look) ____________________ for a long time.

2c *Used To* + Base Verb and *Would* + Base Verb

Student Book p. 44

15 Practice

Underline the correct forms in parentheses.

A.

1. When my grandparents were young, many people (had smoked / used to smoke) in public places.
2. Where (did people use to / people would) smoke?
3. People (would smoke / use to smoke) in almost any public place, including restaurants and movie theaters.
4. They (wouldn't think / didn't use to think) that smoking was dangerous.
5. My grandfather (would start / started) smoking back in college.
6. At that time, students and professors (had / would have) very different attitudes about cigarettes.
7. Some students (used to light / were used to light) cigarettes in the classroom!

B.

1. Romance today is different from in the past. In the 1940s, a man (used to "court" / was used to "court") a woman.
2. A true gentleman (would used to bring / would bring) a woman flowers every time he came to see her.
3. A woman (would try / used to trying) to win his love with clever conversation and charm, not just with appearance.
4. My grandmother (won / used to win) my grandfather's heart this way in 1941.
5. In that same year, he (used to ask / asked) her to marry him.

C.

1. In the past, people (used to dress / used to dressing) more formally than they do now.
2. In the 1940s, my grandmother (used to wear / wore) a skirt to work every day.
3. She also (wouldn't leave / didn't leave) her house without a matching hat and purse.
4. She (wouldn't wear / didn't wear) flat shoes with skirts.
5. She (used to walk / walked) everywhere in heels.
6. My grandfather (used to go / went) to work in a suit every day.
7. He (would work / worked) in the office from 8:00 till 6:00 five days a week.
8. Until the 1960s, most people (didn't use to go / use to not go) outside without a hat.

16 Practice

Look at the chart about the business world in the 1930s and the business world today. Write sentences about the 1930s with *used to* or *would* (or *didn't use to / wouldn't*) compared with today. Use the verbs in the chart.

	Businesspeople in the Past	Businesspeople Today
1.	type or write by hand	write on computers
2.	work only in the office	work from anywhere (like home)
3.	don't have good phone service	talk on cell phones with improved technology
4.	do a lot of business in person	don't always meet the people they do business with
5.	write letters	send and receive email
6.	don't dress informally	often wear informal clothes

1. ______________________________,
but now ______________________________.

2. Today, ______________________________,
but in the past, ______________________________.

3. ______________________________,
but these days ______________________________.

4. Now, ______________________________;
in contrast, in the past, ______________________________.

5. ______________________________;
however, today ______________________________.

6. These days, ______________________________,
whereas in the past, ______________________________.

17 Practice

Do you see any changes from the recent past until now? Think about the 1980s or the 1990s. What did you use to do then that you don't do now? What would other people do? Write eight sentences with *used to* and *would*. Use the following verbs and your own ideas.

1. listen to / dance to

____.

2. pay

____.

3. go

____.

4. like

____.

5. wear

____.

6. think

____.

7. *your idea*

____.

8. *your idea*

____.

9. *your idea*

____.

10. *your idea*

____.

SELF-TEST

A Choose the best answer, A, B, C, or D, to complete the sentence. Mark your answer by darkening the oval with the same letter.

1. Maria failed the test. She ____________ for it.

A. didn't use to study Ⓐ Ⓑ Ⓒ Ⓓ
B. wasn't studying
C. hadn't studied
D. wasn't used to studying

2. While the children ____________, the parents relaxed.

A. had played Ⓐ Ⓑ Ⓒ Ⓓ
B. were playing
C. used to play
D. would play

3. Amy ____________ at a restaurant, but now she works in an office.

A. was used to working Ⓐ Ⓑ Ⓒ Ⓓ
B. use to work
C. would work
D. used to work

4. How many miles ____________ in that old car?

A. had he driven Ⓐ Ⓑ Ⓒ Ⓓ
B. he drove
C. had he been driving
D. he was driving

5. By the time the airplane landed, the passengers ____________ for ten hours.

A. flew Ⓐ Ⓑ Ⓒ Ⓓ
B. had been flying
C. were flying
D. would fly

6. What TV show ____________ last night?

A. have they watched Ⓐ Ⓑ Ⓒ Ⓓ
B. did they watch
C. had they watched
D. they were watching

7. The mother did everything she could, but her baby ____________ crying.

A. wouldn't stop Ⓐ Ⓑ Ⓒ Ⓓ
B. didn't use to stop
C. hadn't stopped
D. wasn't stopping

8. The family was eating breakfast when somebody ____________ at the door.

A. was knocking Ⓐ Ⓑ Ⓒ Ⓓ
B. had been knocking
C. knocked
D. had knocked

9. How long ____________ by the time I got home?

A. were you waiting Ⓐ Ⓑ Ⓒ Ⓓ
B. did you wait
C. did you use to wait
D. had you been waiting

10. Tim: Were you talking to me?
John: No, I ____________. I was talking to Bob.

A. didn't Ⓐ Ⓑ Ⓒ Ⓓ
B. wasn't
C. hadn't
D. wouldn't

B Find the underlined word or phrase, A, B, C, or D, that is incorrect. Mark your answer by darkening the oval with the same letter.

1. I drink [A] coffee these days [B], but I didn't [C] used to [D].

Ⓐ Ⓑ Ⓒ Ⓓ

2. While [A] the woman had been [B] leaving [C] her house, the telephone rang [D].

Ⓐ Ⓑ Ⓒ Ⓓ

3. Before she became [A] a dentist, Lisa had [B] been [C] being [D] an ice skater.

Ⓐ Ⓑ Ⓒ Ⓓ

4. He had [A] been running [B] twelve miles when [C] he suddenly collapsed [D].

Ⓐ Ⓑ Ⓒ Ⓓ

5. By the time we were arriving [A], the train had [B] already [C] left [D] the station.

Ⓐ Ⓑ Ⓒ Ⓓ

6. He looked [A] healthy because [B] he had been exercise [C] regularly [D].

Ⓐ Ⓑ Ⓒ Ⓓ

7. Why [A] hasn't [B] anyone told us [C] that we needed [D] to be there by 3:00?

Ⓐ Ⓑ Ⓒ Ⓓ

8. The soccer team used to practice [A] six days a week [B] in 1999, but [C] they aren't [D] now.

Ⓐ Ⓑ Ⓒ Ⓓ

9. From the moment [A] the race was starting [B], the black horse led [C] all the others [D].

Ⓐ Ⓑ Ⓒ Ⓓ

10. Her grandparents were [A] used to [B] live [C] in a house, but now they live [D] in an apartment.

Ⓐ Ⓑ Ⓒ Ⓓ

UNIT 3 THE FUTURE

3a *Be Going To* and *Will*

Student Book p. 58

1 Practice

Complete the sentences with the *be going to* or the *will* form of the verbs in parentheses.

A.

Todd: Oh no! I'm sorry. My dog has just eaten the cookies you baked!

Jennifer: Don't worry. I (bake) ___'ll bake___ (1) some more. Do you think your dog (get) ______________ (2) sick from eating all those cookies?

Todd: No, he ______________ (3). He (eat) ______________ (4) everything. But I think I (take) ______________ (5) him outside for a walk. He (not, find) ______________ (6) anything interesting to eat out there.

Jennifer: I'm afraid your dog (not, be) ______________ (7) very happy outside. It's really cold. I think it (snow) ______________ (8).

Todd: I'm sure he (be) ______________ (9) fine. He has a lot of fur. That (keep) ______________ (10) him warm.

B.

Kathy: (you, add) ______________ (1) more fruit to the smoothie? I'm afraid the blender (break) ______________ (2). There is already a lot of fruit in there.

Rick: The blender (not, break) ______________ (3). Don't forget, I (be) ______________ (4) a famous chef someday! I know what I'm doing.

Kathy: Yes, but the juice is already at the top of the blender. It (spill) ______________ (5).

Rick: I've been making this recipe for years. I've never had a problem with it before, and I (not, have) ______________ (6) a problem with it now.

Kathy: There (be) ______________ (7) a big mess in the kitchen. I'm sure of it.

Rick: Then I (clean) ______________ (8) it up for you. Now, I (put) ______________ (9) the lid on. Then I (turn on) ______________ (10) the blender. Are you ready? Stand back!

2 Practice

A. Read the information from a brochure about yoga classes. Complete the sentences with *be going to* or *will* and verbs from the list.

be	meet
feel	offer
give	see
help	show
learn	teach
make	

Welcome to Yoga Journeys!

On February 6, Yoga Journeys __is going to offer__ (1) a free class for beginning yoga students. The class ____________ (2) from 1:00 to 2:30 at the main studio on Linden Avenue. Our master teacher, Donna Bliss, ____________ (3) this class.

In this class, you ____________ (4) the basics of yoga positions. With her gentle and supportive teaching style, Donna also ____________ (5) you how to breathe correctly. Because this is an introductory class, she (not) ____________ (6) you do any complicated movements. Don't worry!

Over time, yoga practice ____________ (7) you strength and flexibility. In one class, you probably (not) ____________ (8) instant results. But you ____________ (9) more relaxed after just a few minutes of yoga. Yoga ____________ (10) you to concentrate and to focus.

Our society is becoming more stressful, so yoga ____________ (11) an increasingly important way to manage stress in the future. Take a break from stress. Come join us on a yoga journey!

B. Use the prompts to write yes/no and wh- questions. Use the *be going to* or the *will* form of the verb. Then use information from the reading in Part A to write answers.

1. when / Yoga Journeys / offer / a free class

   Question: *When is Yoga Journeys going to offer a free class?*

   Answer: *Yoga Journeys is going to (OR will) offer a free class on February 6, from 1:00-2:30.*

2. where / the class / meet

   Question: ______________________________?

   Answer: ______________________________.

3. who / teach / the class

   Question: ______________________________?

   Answer: ______________________________.

4. what / you / learn / in this class

   Question: ______________________________?

   Answer: ______________________________.

5. the teacher / make you learn / any complicated movements

   Question: ______________________________?

   Answer: ______________________________.

6. a yoga class / make / you / stronger and more flexible

   Question: ______________________________?

   Answer: ______________________________.

7. you / feel / strong and flexible / after just one class

   Question: ______________________________?

   Answer: ______________________________.

8. how / you / feel / after just a few minutes of yoga

   Question: ______________________________?

   Answer: ______________________________.

9. why / yoga / be / an increasingly important way to manage stress

   Question: ______________________________?

   Answer: ______________________________.

3 Practice

Think of a sport, hobby, or activity that you enjoy. Imagine you are going to offer a free class on this activity. Write six sentences using *be going to* + verb or *will* + verb. Then use the sentences to create a brochure like the one in Practice 2.

1. ______________________________
2. ______________________________
3. ______________________________
4. ______________________________
5. ______________________________
6. ______________________________

3b Time Clauses and Conditional Sentences in the Future

Student Book p. 62

4 Practice

Marco is traveling in Italy. Match the information in column A with the information in column B to make complete sentences from his letter home.

Dear Mom and Dad,

A

__*i*__ **1.** I can't believe it! When this train stops,

_____ **2.** While I'm traveling to Rome,

_____ **3.** I'm going to leave my backpack at the hotel

_____ **4.** After I check in to my hotel,

_____ **5.** I won't leave Rome

_____ **6.** I'll think of you both

_____ **7.** I'll buy nice gifts for everyone

_____ **8.** Unless I save some money,

_____ **9.** I'm going to take the train to Naples

_____ **10.** I'll write to you again

B

a. until I see the Trevi Fountain.

b. if I have enough money.

c. as soon as I get to Naples.

d. after I spend three days in Rome.

e. I won't be able to afford a ticket to Naples.

f. I'm going to visit the Coliseum.

g. before I go sightseeing in Rome.

h. while I'm eating gelato on the Spanish Steps.

i. I'll be in Rome!

j. I'll write to you about my plans.

5 Practice

Marco's parents are talking about his letter from Italy. Use the prompts to write their questions about Marco's travel plans. Write each question two ways: once with the time or condition clause at the beginning and once with it at the end. Use correct punctuation.

1. What / do / when / arrive / in Rome

   What is Marco going to do when he arrives in Rome?

   When Marco arrives in Rome, what is he going to do?

2. Where / go / after / leave / Rome

   ____

   ____

3. When / write / to us / after / visit / Naples

   ____

   ____

4. What / do / if / spend / all his money

   ____

   ____

5. How / ask for help / if / get lost

   ____

   ____

6. If / become sick / who / call

   ____

   ____

6 Practice

What are your plans for the future? Complete the sentences with a time clause, a condition clause, or a main clause.

1. As soon as I finish school, ______________________________.
2. If I have enough money, ______________________________.
3. I won't get a job ______________________________.
4. Until I improve my English, ______________________________.
5. Once I get a job, ______________________________.
6. While I'm living here, ______________________________.
7. After I've been living here a while, ______________________________.
8. I'll be very happy ______________________________.
9. I'll feel sad ______________________________.
10. Before ______________________________, ______________________________.
11. ______________________________ if ______________________________.
12. When ______________________________, ______________________________.

3c Present with Future Meaning

Student Book p. 66

7 Practice

Complete the sentences with the present progressive or the simple present.

Amy: When (the store, open) ___does the store open___(1)?

Salesclerk: We (open) ________(2) at 10:00 every day. Can you come back?

Amy: I can't. It's 9:15 now, and I (start) ________(3) work at 9:30.

Salesclerk: This evening we (stay) ________(4) open until 7:30 because of the big shoe sale we (have) ________(5). Can you come back later today?

Amy: No. Today I (leave) ________(6) town right after work.

Salesclerk: The sale (continue) ________(7) all through the weekend. You could return on Saturday or Sunday.

Amy: Actually, I (go) ________(8) out of town for the whole weekend.

Salesclerk: I see. What day (come, you) ________(9) back?

Amy: I (return) ________(10) on Monday. But I've just remembered — I (not, work) ________(11) that day. (you, still, sell) ________(12) shoes at 40% off next week?

Salesclerk: No, we (not, be) ________(13). The sale (end) ________(14) on Monday.

8 Practice

Keiko and Michael are making plans. Use the information to write sentences about their scheduled activities and arrangements. Use the simple present or the present progressive. The time clause may be at the beginning or the end of the sentence.

Around 6:30:	Michael picks Keiko up at home.
At 7:00:	Eat dinner at the Boston Bistro.
At 8:15:	Movie starts.
At 10:00:	Movie ends.
Around 10:15:	Go out for coffee and dessert.
After coffee and dessert:	Drive to a friend's party.
No later than 11:30:	Michael drives Keiko home.
At 8:00 A.M. the next day:	Keiko works.

1. *Michael is picking Keiko up at home around 6:30.*
2. ______________________________
3. ______________________________
4. ______________________________
5. ______________________________
6. ______________________________
7. ______________________________
8. ______________________________

3d The Future Progressive

Student Book p. 69

9 Practice

Woodland College is having an open house for new students tomorrow. Use the schedule and prompts to write questions and answers about what will be happening at the open house. Use the future progressive tense.

Woodland College Open House Agenda

8:00	Students and parents arrive at the college.
8:30	Students and parents eat a continental breakfast in the cafeteria.
9:00	Students and parents register for open house.
9:30	The president addresses new students and their parents in the auditorium.
10:00	Morning activities start.
11:30	Students give tours of the campus.
12:00	Professors meet with parents and students at lunch to talk about their classes.
1:00	Dr. Linda Hale lectures about the importance of college today.
2:00	Dr. Ed Mesler leads a discussion about choosing a major.
3:00	Kathleen Henry talks about financial aid.

1. when / students and parents / arrive at the college

Question: *When will students and parents be arriving at the college?*

Answer: *They will be arriving at the college by 8:00.*

2. when / students and parents / eat breakfast

Question: ______________________________

Answer: ______________________________

3. when / students and parents / register for the open house

Question: ____

Answer: ____

4. where / the president / address new students

Question: ____

Answer: ____

5. at what time / morning activities / start

Question: ____

Answer: ____

6. who / give tours / of the campus

Question: ____

Answer: ____

7. what / happen / at lunch

Question: ____

Answer: ____

8. what / Dr. Hale / lecture about

Question: ____

Answer: ____

9. what / Dr. Mesler / lead a discussion about

Question: ____

Answer: ____

10. who / talk about / financial aid

Question: ____

Answer: ____

10 Practice

Shiva and his mother are at the Woodland College Open House. Complete their conversation with *will* + base verb or the future progressive of the verbs in parentheses.

Shiva: The campus tour (start) will be starting (1) in a few minutes.

Mother: Oh, good. I think I (go) ________ (2) on the tour with you.

Shiva: Actually, the schedule says there (be) ________ (3) two tours at the same time: one for parents and one for students.

Mother: Oh, ok. Then I guess I (take) ________ (4) the tour for parents.

Shiva: (you, go) ________ (5) back to work after that? Or (you, stay) ________ (6) for lunch?

Mother: I thought I would go back to work. But now I think I (stay) ________ (7). If I miss lunch, I (not, get) ________ (8) a chance to meet your professors. I'd like to see what professors you (have) ________ (9) in the fall.

Shiva: You don't have to stay. I (tell) ________ (10) you about them when I come home.

Mother: I'd really like to stay. In just a few weeks you (go) ________ (11) to classes, and I (not, see) ________ (12) you as often.

11 Practice

Imagine that you are planning a vacation for the people in the photograph. Tell them where they will be going and what they will be doing at the following dates and times. Use the future progressive. You may use ideas from the list or your own.

check in to hotel	hike in the Grand Pitons
dine by candlelight	lie on a beach
fly to St. Lucia	miss the snow and cold

1. On Saturday, January 15, you ________________________ at 8:00 A.M.
2. At 11:30 A.M., ________________________.
3. ________________________ by this time tomorrow.
4. ________________________ in the afternoon.
5. In the evening, ________________________.
6. ________________________ at the end of the day.

3e Other Expressions of the Future; The Future in the Past

Student Book p. 72

12 Practice

Complete the sentences using *be to* or *be about to* + the verbs in parentheses.

1. Gabriel Torres (finish) _is about to finish_ his latest painting.

2. He (paint) ______________________________ the last detail.

3. The painting (be) ______________________________ displayed in a famous art gallery.

4. It (sell) ______________________________ for nearly $50,000.

5. When the painting is sold, the money (help) ______________________________ start an art program for children in New York City.

6. Gabriel (call) ______________________________ his agent and tell him the good news.

7. His agent thinks Gabriel's art career (become) ______________________________ very successful.

13 Practice

Gabriel had just finished his painting when something happened to change his plans. Complete the sentences using *was/were about to* + the verbs in parentheses.

1. Gabriel (paint) ______________________________ the last part when he heard a noise outside.

2. His five-year-old daughter (knock) ______________________________ on the door, but instead, she ran into the room.

3. Gabriel (move) ______________________________ away from the painting. However, surprised by his daughter, he moved toward it. Red paint sprayed on the canvas.

4. His daughter (laugh) ______________________________, but when she saw Gabriel's face, she started to cry.

5. Gabriel's wife came in. She and Gabriel (yell) ______________________________ at their daughter, but they hugged her instead.

6. They (tell) ______________________________ her that she had done something wrong, but they realized she was too young to understand.

7. Gabriel (call) ______________________________ the agent and tell him the painting would not be done, but then he changed his mind.

8. He (start) ______________________________ a new painting, but then he decided that the red paint made the painting more interesting.

14 Practice

For each photo, write three sentences using the prompts and a verb of your choice.

A.

1. (*be to* or *be about to*)

____

____

________________________________.

2. (*was/were going to* + verb)

____.

3. (*plan, intend, decide,* or *mean* + infinitive)

____.

B.

1. (*be to* or *be about to*)

____

____

____

______________________________________.

2. (*was/were going to* + verb)

____

______________________________________.

____.

3. (*plan, intend, decide,* or *mean* + infinitive)

____.

3f The Future Perfect and The Future Perfect Progressive

Student Book p. 75

15 Practice

Melissa is about to graduate. Complete the sentences using the simple present, the future perfect, or the future perfect progressive and the verbs in parentheses.

1. By the end of the day, Melissa (graduate) _will have graduated_.
2. By the end of the ceremony, her parents (see) ________________ her receive her diploma.
3. Before she (graduate) ________________, she (practice) ________________ the ceremony with her classmates twice.
4. By the end of the ceremony, she (wear) ________________ her cap and gown for two hours.
5. By Sunday, Melissa (attend) ________________ three graduation parties.
6. Also by then, she (receive) ________________ many cards and gifts.
7. Who (her, send) ________________ cards and gifts?
8. She has many relatives from far away. They (not, come) ________________ by then.
9. By the time she (start) ________________ the fall semester at college, she (be) ________________ away from high school for four months.
10. She (work) ________________ for four months before she (go) ________________ to college.
11. Before she (quit) ________________ her summer job, she (save)

________________________ her money for college for four months.

12. Hopefully, she (save) ________________________ at least $1,000 by the end of August.

13. Meanwhile, by this time next year, what (her parents, do) ________________ ?

14. They (prepare) ________________________ for another graduation.

15. Her younger sister (finish) ________________________ high school by May of next year!

16 Practice

Imagine that you will live to be 100. What do you think you will have done (or not done) by your 100th birthday? Write three sentences using the future perfect and three sentences using the future perfect progressive.

____

____

____

____

____

____

17 Practice

Read these sentences about the future. Write *C* next to the sentence if the tense is used correctly. Write *I* if it is used incorrectly.

_____ **1.** How long they will have been traveling in Asia?

_____ **2.** By the end of the summer, my little brother will have been reading 25 books.

_____ **3.** Where will everyone be working after the company closes?

_____ **4.** The mayor is give a speech at 3:00 today.

_____ **5.** Jacob will be attending law school next year.

_____ **6.** Will you be being at home tonight, or are you going out?

_____ **7.** If the painters will have finished by 4:00, they will earn more money.

_____ **8.** The boss won't call you unless there is a problem.

_____ **9.** I am about to call her, but I couldn't find the phone number.

_____ **10.** Elise will have practicing the piano for three hours by the time her parents come home.

SELF-TEST

A Choose the best answer, A, B, C, or D, to complete the sentence. Mark your answer by darkening the oval with the same letter.

1. I will read the book when I ____________ the time.

A. am going to have (A) (B) (C) (D)
B. will have
C. have
D. am having

2. Hurry up! The class ____________ in five minutes!

A. starts (A) (B) (C) (D)
B. will have started
C. starting
D. will starting

3. Miguel ____________ by the time his brother starts high school.

A. graduated (A) (B) (C) (D)
B. will graduating
C. will has graduated
D. will have graduated

4. They ____________ that car, but they decided not to.

A. are going to buy (A) (B) (C) (D)
B. are about to buy
C. will be buying
D. were about to buy

5. Tom: Oh, no! I left my books in the restaurant.
Lisa: Wait here. ____________ them for you.

A. I get (A) (B) (C) (D)
B. I'll get
C. I'm going to get
D. I'm getting

6. Chris has been driving without a break. He ____________ in Ohio by 6:00.

A. is going to arrive (A) (B) (C) (D)
B. will arrived
C. arrives
D. will arriving

7. Who ____________ if you need money?

A. will you have called (A) (B) (C) (D)
B. you will call
C. will you call
D. are you calling

8. The neighbors ____________ back from vacation until Sunday.

A. aren't coming (A) (B) (C) (D)
B. are not come
C. not be coming
D. aren't going to come

9. By the time Sara ____________ the gym, she will have been exercising for two hours.

A. is leaving (A) (B) (C) (D)
B. has left
C. will have left
D. leaves

10. I can't meet you at 1:00. ____________ lunch with my boss at that time.

A. I'm eat (A) (B) (C) (D)
B. I'll be eating
C. I will have eaten
D. I will have been eating

B Find the underlined word or phrase, A, B, C, or D, that is incorrect. Mark your answer by darkening the oval with the same letter.

1. Jessica is saving (A) all her money because (B) she will plan (C) to travel (D) in Europe.

Ⓐ Ⓑ Ⓒ Ⓓ

2. Will (A) she has (B) finished (C) the test by the end (D) of the class?

Ⓐ Ⓑ Ⓒ Ⓓ

3. Emily was about to (A) buying (B) the shoes, but she decided (C) they were (D) too expensive.

Ⓐ Ⓑ Ⓒ Ⓓ

4. The invitation says (A) that the wedding will to (B) begin (C) at exactly (D) 6:00.

Ⓐ Ⓑ Ⓒ Ⓓ

5. By the time (A) the baseball game ends (B), we will (C) have been spending (D) all our money.

Ⓐ Ⓑ Ⓒ Ⓓ

6. They start (A) the meeting as soon as (B) everyone has (C) arrived (D).

Ⓐ Ⓑ Ⓒ Ⓓ

7. What (A) does Ken want (B) to do if (C) he will become (D) president of the club?

Ⓐ Ⓑ Ⓒ Ⓓ

8. The bus is departing (A) at 9:00 every (B) morning, and it (C) returns (D) at 3:00 each afternoon.

Ⓐ Ⓑ Ⓒ Ⓓ

9. How long (A) they will (B) have been talking (C) by the time they hang up (D) the phone?

Ⓐ Ⓑ Ⓒ Ⓓ

10. I predict (A) they are canceling (B) the game if (C) the rain continues (D) all afternoon.

Ⓐ Ⓑ Ⓒ Ⓓ

UNIT 4 NOUNS AND EXPRESSIONS OF QUANTITY

4a Regular and Irregular Plural Nouns

Student Book p. 90

1 Practice

Complete the sentences with the correct form of the nouns in parentheses.

Yesterday, Daryl took his family to the beach, and they had a great time. There were (person) ______(1) playing Frisbee, some (man) ______(2) were fishing, and lots of (child) ______(3) were playing in the sand. The (wave) ______(4) weren't very big, so there were no (surfer) ______(5) in the water. Daryl's family sat in their beach (chair) ______(6) and laid on their (towel) ______(7). After a while, Daryl and his wife walked in the water and got their (foot) ______(8) wet. Near the water, some (dog) ______(9) were chasing some snowy plovers, which are a kind of bird. They are an endangered (species) ______(10).

2 Practice

Read the newscast. Circle the correct form of the verbs in parentheses.

In the news today, five people (was / were)(1) caught trying to break in to a department store downtown. One woman (was / were)(2) later released, but the four men (was / were)(3) held at the police station. The men (is / are)(4) accused of trying to steal radios, CD players, and laptops. The laptops (was / were)(5) found in the back of the men's van. The thieves (hasn't / haven't)(6) spoken to lawyers yet.

3 Practice

Read these sentences. Write *C* next to the sentence if the noun forms are correct. Write *I* if the noun forms are incorrect.

_____ **1.** Doug is studying physics at school.

_____ **2.** When he gets his master's degree, he'll have to write a theses.

_____ **3.** He chose that school because it has the best curriculum.

_____ **4.** The person in his department are brilliant.

_____ **5.** Doug received a memoranda yesterday about his final project.

_____ **6.** He's writing a series of articles for a national magazine.

_____ **7.** His wife is also a scientist. She studies bacteria in cacti and fungus.

_____ **8.** They have a young children.

_____ **9.** Their son just got his first tooth.

_____ **10.** Doug and his wife hope to get good paying job when they finish their degrees.

4 Practice

Complete the sentences with your own words. Use *is* or *are* in your answers.

1. My teeth ____.

2. The media in my country ____________________________________,

so the news ____.

3. ______________________________ an endangered species in my country.

4. Blue jeans ____.

5. Businesspeople ____.

6. A 60-year-old man ____.

7. Five-year-old children ____.

4b Possessive Nouns; Possessive Phrases with *Of*

Student Book p. 93

5 Practice

Read the sentences. Answer the questions with *one* or *more than one*.

1. **a.** The men's hobbies are expensive.
   How many men have hobbies?
   more than one

   b. The man's hobbies are expensive.
   How many men have hobbies?
   ____

2. **a.** The room's furniture needs replacing.
   How many rooms should get new furniture?
   ____

   b. The rooms' furniture needs replacing.
   How many rooms should get new furniture?
   ____

3. **a.** I can't find the child's toys.
   How many children are missing toys? ______________________

   b. I can't find the children's toys.
   How many children are missing toys? ______________________

4. **a.** The boys' projects are almost finished.
   How many boys are almost finished? ______________________

   b. The boy's projects are almost finished.
   How many boys are almost finished? ______________________

5. **a.** The baby's blankets are dirty.
   How many babies have dirty blankets? ______________________

   b. The babies' blankets are dirty.
   How many babies have dirty blankets? ______________________

6. **a.** The students' homework is too difficult.
   How many students have difficult homework? ______________________

   b. The student's homework is too difficult.
   How many students have difficult homework? ______________________

6 Practice

Read the conversations. Rewrite sentence B, adding the possessive noun that is missing.

1. **A:** Whose CD is that?

   B. It's Scott's. It's Scott's CD ______________________.

2. **A:** Whose car is that?

   B: It's Leslie's. ______________________.

3. **A:** Whose responsibility will it be?

   B: It'll be the city's. ______________________.

4. **A:** Whose turn is it to pay for lunch?

   B: It's Cheryl's. ______________________.

5. **A:** Whose idea was it to put salt in the sugar bowl?

   B: It was Alex's. ______________________.

6. **A:** Whose locker was broken into?

   B: Patricia's. ______________________.

7. **A:** Whose material are you using?

   B: The department's. ______________________.

8. **A:** Whose database will we be accessing?

   B: Accounting's. ______________________.

7 Practice

Use apostrophes or *of* and the words in parentheses to complete the sentences.

My (neighbor, house) ______________ (1) caught on fire last night. The fire started (in the front, house) ______________ (2). The (electrical system, house) ______________ (3) was faulty. My neighbor lost (her mother, jewelry) ______________ (4) and (her children, photos) ______________ (5), but thankfully no one was hurt.

8 Practice

Read these sentences. Write *C* next to the sentence if the apostrophe or *of* is correct. Write *I* if it is incorrect.

______ **1.** Tomorrow homework is to read chapter two.

______ **2.** We will hear Maria presentation.

______ **3.** Let's look at today assignment.

______ **4.** The date of the exam will be announced next week.

______ **5.** The name the next unit is Ancient Greek History.

______ **6.** IT installed the laser jet printer in the corner of the room.

______ **7.** Has Mr. Monroe turned in his letter resignation?

______ **8.** The erosion hillside is now threatening the subdivisions below it.

9 Practice

Write sentences using apostrophes or *of*, the words in parentheses, and your ideas.

1. The (name, this book) is ______________________.

*The name of this book is Grammar Form and Function*______.

2. My (best friend, name) is ______________________.

____.

3. My (parent, taste) in clothes is ______________________.

____.

4. My (instructor, name) is ______________________.

____.

5. My (family, last vacation) was ______________________.

____.

6. The (streets, my city) are ______________________.

____.

7. ______________________ is my favorite (time, the year).

____.

8. ______________________ is the (name, my favorite book).

____.

4c Compound Nouns

Student Book p. 97

10 Practice

Match each group of words on the left with the word on the right that fits to make compound nouns.

1. _____: hat, cut, doll — **a.** water
2. _____: spray, brush, cut — **b.** car
3. _____: bulb, switch, pole — **c.** music
4. _____: graphics, programmer, science — **d.** coffee
5. _____: mechanic, door, seat — **e.** light
6. _____: fall, glass, bottle — **f.** paper
7. _____: lesson, teacher, video — **g.** hair
8. _____: table, pot, machine — **h.** computer

11 Practice

Complete the sentences with compound nouns using the information.

1. The tour was three hours long. It was a *three-hour tour*.
2. The girl is seven years old. She's a ______________________.
3. The semester is 15 weeks long. It's a ______________________.
4. Her latest book is 600 pages long. It is a ______________________.
5. The flight was 16 hours long. It was a ______________________.
6. The meal was three courses. It was a ______________________.
7. The bottle of wine cost six dollars. It was a ______________________.
8. Our final paper is going to be ten pages long. It's going to be a ______________________.
9. We don't have school on Monday. Our weekend will be three days long. It's going to be a ______________________.
10. That restaurant has four stars. It must be good. It's a ______________________.

12 Practice

Underline the compound nouns in the following reading.

Nick had wanted to be a race-car driver ever since he was a seven-year-old boy. In high school, he worked part time as an auto mechanic while he took driving lessons. The day he got his driver's license was the happiest one of his life!

Nick bought an old car and worked on it in his spare time. He started racing other boys on country roads outside town. As he won more and more of these races, he became more and more confident. Pretty soon, Nick applied to drive on a professional racetrack.

The day of the race, there was a rainstorm. Huge thunderclouds made the sky black, and the race was cancelled. Nick was disappointed, but he now had a chance to double-check his car. It was a good thing. During his inspection, he noticed his seatbelt wasn't connected well to the base! If he had raced, it could have been very dangerous.

4d Count Nouns and Noncount Nouns

Student Book p. 101

13 Practice

Read these phrases. Write *C* next to the phrase if the article is used correctly. Write *I* if it is used incorrectly.

_____ **1.** a happiness

_____ **2.** an air

_____ **3.** an experience

_____ **4.** a weather

_____ **5.** an iron

_____ **6.** a glass

_____ **7.** a sunshine

_____ **8.** two sodas

_____ **9.** a hair

_____ **10.** a rice

14 Practice

Read the recipe for brownies. Circle the count nouns. Underline the noncount nouns.

from the kitchen of ____________________

Brownies

$\frac{1}{2}$ cup butter

2 squares of chocolate

1 cup of sugar

2 eggs

1 teaspoon vanilla

$\frac{3}{4}$ cup flour

$\frac{1}{2}$ cup nuts

Melt the butter and chocolate together. Remove from heat. Stir in sugar. Add eggs and vanilla. Mix gently until combined. Add flour and nuts. Put mixture in a square cake pan and bake for 30 minutes at 350°.

15 Practice

Circle the correct verbs in parentheses.

1. Geography (isn't / aren't) very interesting to me.
2. Medicine (is / are) a popular major at my university.
3. My new glasses (is / are) already broken!
4. Bad experiences (is / are) a part of life.
5. Chocolate (is / are) good for you.
6. Education (is / are) very important.
7. The good times I had in college (was / were) some of my happiest moments.
8. Time (goes / go) quickly.
9. Gasoline (has been / have been) very expensive lately.
10. The two cups of coffee I had this morning (is / are) making me nervous.

16 Practice

Add two more items to each of the noncount noun lists.

Languages	Natural Forces	Recreation
Portuguese	wind	soccer
______	______	______
______	______	______

Abstract Nouns	Liquid	Particles
love	milk	sand
______	______	______
______	______	______

17 Practice

Complete the sentences with *much, many, little,* or *few.*

A. Art Director: You don't have ______ (1) ideas.

Artist: I didn't have ______ (2) time to do this. ______ (3) artists could meet this deadline. I had ______ (4) warning.

Art Director: This is an important client. ______ (5) other companies want its business.

B. Mia: My parrot isn't doing ______ (1) talking today.

Tawni: Do you think he's depressed? He has very ______ (2) room to walk around in that cage.

Mia: No, this is just his traveling cage. His cage at home is huge. ______ (3) birds have such luxury!

Tawni: Oh, so where's he going?

Mia: To my best friend's apartment. He's gone there ______ (4) times before. He loves to go visit, so he'll probably start talking again once we get there.

18 Practice

Complete the sentences with your own ideas.

1. Students have too much __________________ and too little __________________.
2. They have too many __________________ and too few __________________.
3. Parents have too many __________________ and too few __________________.
4. In the winter, there is too much ________________ and too little ________________.

4e *Some* and *Any*

Student Book p. 104

19 Practice

Circle the correct words in parentheses.

Leonard: Come on over. We can get (some / any)[1] Chinese food.

Ziggy: There's never (some / any)[2] parking in your neighborhood.

Leonard: Take the bus. There isn't (some / any)[3] traffic this time of day.

Ziggy: Okay. Should I bring (some / any)[4] drinks?

Leonard: Well, I have (some / any)[5] bananas and yogurt and was thinking of making (some / any)[6] smoothies.

Ziggy: Okay. How about if I bring (some / any)[7] strawberries? Oh, and I've also got (some / any)[8] new CDs to show you.

Leonard: Great.

20 Practice

Read these sentences. Write *C* next to the sentence if *some* or *any* is used correctly. Write *I* if it is used incorrectly.

_____ **1.** The team finished the project without some problems.

_____ **2.** The kids still have some homework to do.

_____ **3.** Dr. Walker seldom has any time for hobbies.

_____ **4.** Darlene's lost weight. She hardly has some clothes to wear.

_____ **5.** She needs to buy some new shoes, too.

_____ **6.** We have to water the garden because we haven't had some rain.

_____ **7.** If you have your own business, you rarely take some vacations.

_____ **8.** You can wear my sunglasses. I have any extra ones in the car.

21 Practice

Complete the sentences with *some* if the speaker expects a "yes" answer. Complete the sentences with *any* if the speaker has no expectation.

1. (I need tape, but I don't know if you have tape.)

Do you have __any__ tape?

2. (I think you'll let me borrow money.)

Could I borrow ____________ money?

3. (Your friend is having a party. You think she needs help.)

Do you need ____________ help?

4. (You don't know if your friend has enough food for the party.)

Should I bring ____________ snacks?

5. (You don't know if other people from work are going to be at the party.)

Will ____________ people from work be there?

6. (Your friend doesn't have enough CDs. You think she would like music at the party.)

Do you want me to bring ____________ music?

22 Practice

Write *a, b,* or *c* beside each sentence to identify which meaning of *any* is being used.

_____	**1.** I can meet you any time you like.	**a.**	Negative meaning
_____	**2.** There's hardly any tea left!	**b.**	No expectation
_____	**3.** Our math teacher doesn't have any patience.	**c.**	It doesn't matter which one
_____	**4.** Any kind of cake is fine with me.		
_____	**5.** Are there any more dishes in the sink?		
_____	**6.** She never has any money.		
_____	**7.** Did you have any pets growing up?		
_____	**8.** Jake will take any job he's offered.		

4f *Much, Many, A Lot Of, A Few, Few, A Little,* and *Little*

Student Book p. 106

23 Practice

Complete the sentences with *a little, a few,* or *a lot of.* More than one answer may be correct.

Anne: My wallet was stolen!

Mike: Did you have ______(1)______ money in it?

Anne: No, only ______(2)______, but I had ______(3)______ pictures and credit cards.

Mike: When did this happen?

Anne: Only ______(4)______ hours ago.

Mike: Have you called the police?

Anne: Yes, I talked to them ______(5)______ while ago.

Mike: Do you need ______(6)______ money right now? I can lend you some.

Anne: No, thanks, Mike. I have ______(7)______ dollars at home.

24 Practice

Complete the sentences with *much, many, a few, few, a little, little,* or *a lot of.*

My nephew is staying with me for the summer, and he's driving me crazy. We're having ______ (1) problems, not many. He tried doing his laundry and put too ______ (2) soap in the washing machine. There were bubbles and water everywhere! He gets too ______ (3) phone calls late at night, and he makes too ______ (4) noise. I'm getting very ______ (5) sleep. I still have ______ (6) patience, but I'm left with ______ (7) options. ______ (8) things are going to have to change.

25 Practice

What does each sentence mean? Answer the questions.

1. I have a few friends.

   Do I have friends? Yes, you have some friends, but not a lot of friends.

2. My brother has few friends.

   Does he have friends? ______.

3. The students have very little time to finish the project.

   How much time do the students have? ______.

4. Very few people are still in the office at this hour.

   How many people are still working? ______.

5. There's a little soap left.

   Can I do laundry? ______.

6. We found a little money in the sofa!

   How much money did they find? ______.

7. The director has made few changes to the proposal.

   Has the proposal been changed a lot? ______.

8. We're having a few friends over for dinner.

   How many people will be at dinner? ______.

4g *Each, Each (One) Of, Every, Every One Of, Both, Both Of, All,* and *All Of*

Student Book p. 109

26 Practice

Katie bought a new PDA two months ago. Read the paragraph and circle the correct expressions in parentheses.

I have trouble with this thing (each / every) [1] day. (Each / Every) [2] time I use it, I have to restart it. I have spoken to two customer service representatives, and (each / every) [3] one has told me something different! My husband has the same machine, and (all of / both of) [4] us are frustrated. (All / Every) [5] my friends love their PDAs and never have any problems with them. Today mine crashed, and I can't access the information. (Every one of / Each) [6] my addresses is in it. I think I'm going to return (all of / both of) [7] ours to the store.

27 Practice

Complete the sentences with *both, every,* or *all.*

1. Sharon's been to that doctor twice. ____________________ times, he's kept her waiting for an hour.
2. ____________________ time she tries to talk to him, he's busy.
3. He laughed at ____________________ my jokes, and I told him a lot of them.
4. ____________________ meal on the menu was too expensive.

5. Our daughter's pet hamster kept us awake ________________ night.

6. Luanne can write with ________________ hands.

7. When Juan won the lottery, ________________ of his money problems disappeared.

8. ________________ Alan and Jan have agreed to sign the petition.

9. ________________ one of the people in that room was angry.

10. ________________ the exercises in the book are easy.

28 Practice

Complete the sentences with your own ideas.

1. Both of my eyes ____.

2. Both of my parents ____.

3. All of my friends ____.

4. Each one of my teachers ____.

5. Every one of my classmates ____.

6. Both of my shoes ____.

7. All children ____.

8. Every newspaper in my country ____.

9. Every person needs ____.

10. All of the people in the world ____.

SELF-TEST

A Choose the best answer, A, B, C, or D, to complete the sentence. Mark your answer by darkening the oval with the same letter.

1. My aunt never had any _____.

   A. childs (A) (B) (C) (D)
   B. child's
   C. children's
   D. children

2. When Matthew was in high school, mathematics _____ his favorite subject.

   A. was (A) (B) (C) (D)
   B. were
   C. are
   D. is

3. Last _____ fashions were influenced by hip-hop.

   A. year (A) (B) (C) (D)
   B. year's
   C. years
   D. of year

4. The neighbors bought a _____ house.

   A. 100-year-old (A) (B) (C) (D)
   B. 100-years-old
   C. 100-year's-old
   D. 100-year

5. Pollution in the city _____ in recent years.

   A. are decreased (A) (B) (C) (D)
   B. have decreased
   C. has decreased
   D. were decreased

6. There weren't _____ people injured at the concert.

   A. much (A) (B) (C) (D)
   B. any
   C. some
   D. few

7. My country has very _____ iron, so we import it.

   A. much (A) (B) (C) (D)
   B. many
   C. little
   D. few

8. We rarely get _____ rain in the summer here.

   A. much (A) (B) (C) (D)
   B. many
   C. little
   D. few

9. David works out _____ day.

   A. all of (A) (B) (C) (D)
   B. every
   C. each
   D. both

10. We can't bake a cake. We have too _____ sugar.

    A. many (A) (B) (C) (D)
    B. few
    C. a little
    D. little

B Find the underlined word or phrase, A, B, C, or D, that is incorrect. Mark your answer by darkening the oval with the same letter.

1. We can see some sheep (A), man (B), women (C), children, and geese (D) in the painting.

   Ⓐ Ⓑ Ⓒ Ⓓ

2. Both of (A) the three plays we saw were (B) good. The name of one (C) was *The Time of Your Life*. It was Ted's (D) favorite.

   Ⓐ Ⓑ Ⓒ Ⓓ

3. Mollie took her two-year-old (A) twins on a five-hour (B) trip to Boston. Both (C) days that weekend, she didn't get some (D) rest.

   Ⓐ Ⓑ Ⓒ Ⓓ

4. Al has a driver's license (A), so he's taking us to the bookstore (B). First, I need to get a little (C) money. We don't have few (D) time.

   Ⓐ Ⓑ Ⓒ Ⓓ

5. They didn't have any (A) oranges at the store, so I got some (B) bananas. I also got a few (C) cheese and a little (D) juice.

   Ⓐ Ⓑ Ⓒ Ⓓ

6. Each people (A) must have a ticket. You cannot use another person's (B) ticket, but you can use the same ticket all (C) day. Let's go over a few (D) rules.

   Ⓐ Ⓑ Ⓒ Ⓓ

7. Athletics is (A) an important part of school. Every (B) student (C) should do few (D) exercise.

   Ⓐ Ⓑ Ⓒ Ⓓ

8. I'm washing jeans (A), short (B), and pajamas (C). There's a little (D) hot water if you need to take a shower.

   Ⓐ Ⓑ Ⓒ Ⓓ

9. We had a four-hour (A) dinner. Each of us (B) had fun, and we told a lot of (C) jokes, but I don't remember the name's restaurant (D).

   Ⓐ Ⓑ Ⓒ Ⓓ

10. Many exercises (A) in this book is (B) easy, and a few (C) exercises are (D) fun.

    Ⓐ Ⓑ Ⓒ Ⓓ

UNIT 5 PRONOUNS AND ARTICLES

5a Subject and Object Pronouns; Possessive Adjectives; and Possessive Pronouns

Student Book p. 122

1 Practice

Circle the correct subject, object, possessive pronoun, or possessive adjective.

A. Rich and Sue are discussing their wedding reception.

Sue: Let's put (your / yours)[1] parents next to (my / mine)[2].

Rich: But (my / mine)[3] mother doesn't really know (your / yours)[4].

Sue: I know, but I don't know where else to seat (her / hers)[5].

B. George Washington Carver was the first African American to graduate from what is now Iowa State University. (He / Him)[1] was responsible for many agricultural innovations and discoveries. One of (them / their)[2] was the invention of peanut butter. No one (know / knows)[3] exactly when (he / him)[4] was born, but it was around 1865. (He / His)[5] parents were slaves.

C. (She / Her)[1] said that (her / hers)[2] soccer team had just won the championship match. The trophy is (their / theirs)[3] for the first time. The team and coaches are already planning for next year. (Them / They)[4] want to be sure that the championship trophy stays with (they / them)[5].

D. A wife and husband have just moved into a new house.

Wife: What's (our / ours)[1] new phone number?

Husband: It's 555-8765.

Wife: No, it's not. That's (our / ours)[2] old one.

2 Practice

Complete the sentences with possessive adjectives or pronouns *(my, mine, her, hers, his, our, ours, their, theirs)*.

A. Sarah: I don't want any dessert. You can have __________(1).

Ryan: Thanks, but I think __________(2) dessert is going to be enough.

B. Jenna Lee has just had a job interview. The interviewers are discussing her.

Donna: What did you think of the candidate?

Leroy: __________(1) ideas are interesting.

Donna: Do you think __________(2) are better than the other candidates' ideas?

Leroy: Yes, I do, but I'm not sure we can offer __________(3) enough money to leave __________(4) other job.

C. Maureen: When does __________ vacation start?

Jorge: We leave next Saturday.

D. Two children are arguing over a toy.

Pete: Give it back! It's __________(1).

Ken: No, it's not! It's __________(2).

Mom: Ken! Give it to Pete. It's __________(3).

E. Candace and Joyce have __________ own business.

F. Several people are in the reception area of a public relations firm. The new receptionist goes to ask whose clients they are.

Receptionist: Can anyone tell me whose clients are waiting in reception?

Margo and Miriam: The client in the red suit is __________(1) client. And the client in the black skirt is Norm and Sara's.

Norm and Sara: Yes, the client wearing red is __________(2), and the other one is __________(3).

G. We have an exchange student from Sweden. I'm learning __________(1) language, and he's learning __________(2).

H. Instructor: Please turn off __________ (1) cell phones.

(phone ringing)

Eun Hee: It's not __________ (2). Marc, I think it's __________ (3).

Marc: Oops! Sorry. Yes, it's __________ (4) phone.

3 Practice

Read about Komodo dragons. Complete the sentences with *it's* or *its*.

__________ (1) the largest lizard in the world. __________ (2) found on two Indonesian islands.

__________ (3) teeth can tear easily through flesh.

__________ (4) mouth is filled with bacteria. The infection from a bite can kill __________ (5) prey. __________ (6) long tongue "tastes" the air. A Komodo dragon starts __________ (7) attack when __________ (8) three feet away from __________ (9) victim. __________ (10) an interesting, but ferocious animal.

4 Practice

Answer the questions with *it*.

1. What time is it? __________.
2. What's the weather like? __________.
3. What's the temperature right now? __________.
4. How far is it from your house to your school? __________.
5. How long does it take you to go to school? __________.
6. What's the weather going to be like tomorrow? __________.

5 Practice

Read these sentences. Write *C* next to the sentence if the pronouns and possessive adjectives are used correctly. Write *I* if they are used incorrectly.

_____ **1.** It's ours.

_____ **2.** The baseball fans forgot his tickets.

_____ **3.** Scott critiqued hers project.

_____ **4.** Someone took my parking space!

_____ **5.** Him's drinking some coffee.

_____ **6.** She loves vacations at the beach.

_____ **7.** Everyone needs to bring his or her lunch.

_____ **8.** Talk to she about the plan.

_____ **9.** You can look for apartments online.

_____ **10.** Vicky bought the tickets for we.

6 Practice

Read the sentences. Write *a* next to the sentence if the pronoun is formal. Write *b* if the pronoun is informal. Write *c* if the pronoun is inappropriate.

a. formal
b. informal
c. inappropriate

_____ **1.** Someone left their lights on.

_____ **2.** Everyone is required to clean out his or her locker.

_____ **3.** Did someone call? Did they leave a message?

_____ **4.** If one has time, one should help others less fortunate.

_____ **5.** A good driver has to pay attention to what he's doing.

_____ **6.** No one should say things they don't mean.

_____ **7.** Everyone should clear his desk now.

_____ **8.** A child needs lots of love and support while he or she is growing up.

_____ **9.** Anyone can go, but they need to make a reservation.

_____ **10.** A good teacher should be sensitive to her students' needs.

5b Reflexive Pronouns

Student Book p. 130

7 Practice

Complete the sentences with the correct reflexive pronouns.

A. If you want something done right, do it ____________________.

B. Mom: What happened?!

Henry: Freddy and I tried to fix the car by ________________ (1). Freddy cut ________________ (2) on a sharp piece of metal, and I burned ________________ (3) on the exhaust pipe.

Mom: Are you okay?

Henry: Yes, but we can't fix the car ________________ (4). We'll take it to a mechanic.

C. Carolina: I'm glad you made it to the party! Are you enjoying ______________________ (1)?

Aaron: Of course! I didn't know anyone here, so I introduced ______________________ (2) to Zoe and Ian.

Carolina: Great. Be sure to help ________________ (3) to some cookies. I made them ________________ (4).

8 Practice

Replace the underlined words and phrases with *by* and appropriate reflexive pronouns.

1. On the first day of school, the young friends said, "We can walk to school alone."

On the first day of school, the young friends said, "We can walk to school by ourselves."

2. They wanted to walk to school alone.

____.

3. Some of the most important lessons we learn in life, we have to learn without others.

____.

4. She's doing this exercise <u>alone</u>.

____.

5. He doesn't want to go to the party <u>alone</u>.

____.

6. My three-year-old son wants to get dressed <u>without my help</u>.

____.

7. I don't like living with roommates. I like living <u>alone</u>.

____.

8. Victor and Carol are nervous about driving to Florida <u>alone</u>.

____.

9. You are too dependent on your friends. You should do more things <u>on your own</u>.

____.

10. Father to his two children: Please, go out to the back yard and play <u>with just you two</u> for a few minutes. ____.

9 Practice

Read the sentences. Circle the correct reflexive pronoun in each. If it is incorrect, rewrite the sentence.

1. I didn't invite him! He invited him! ____*He invited himself*____.
2. Our daughter wrote us from Mexico. She's enjoying herself. ____________________.
3. Chen cut himself shaving this morning. ____________________.
4. It's an all-you-can-eat-buffet. Help yourselves. ____________________.
5. I me will help you. ____________________.
6. Our dog taught herself how to open the door to the refrigerator. ____________________.
7. The accident was our fault. We blame us. ____________________.
8. The children locked themselves in the bedroom. We had to call the fire department.

   ____________________.
9. Anne promised her to quit smoking. ____________________.
10. Patrick painted the room him. ____________________.

10 Practice

Complete the sentences with your own ideas and appropriate reflexive pronouns.

1. __I__ don't take care of __myself__ when I __get too busy__.
2. ______ scared ______ when I ______.
3. ______ surprised ______ when she ______.
4. ______ doesn't look at ______ in the mirror because ______.
5. ______ talks to ______ when he ______.
6. ______ drove ______ to the hospital when ______.

5c *Another, Other, Others, The Other,* and *The Others*

Student Book p. 132

11 Practice

Read the sentences. Circle the correct words in parentheses.

1. Some students are coming with us, and (other / others) are meeting us there.
2. Sharon: How's your mom?

   Ron: Some days she's okay, but (other / others) days she's very tired.
3. Jasminda: How long does it take you to get to work?

   Miriam: Most days, just 40 minutes on the subway, but (other / others) days it can take an hour.
4. Walter: I'm looking for an apartment. Can you give me some suggestions?

   Brigitte: Some neighborhoods are pretty nice, but (other / others) are not very safe.

5. Stephanie: How's your new boss?

   Paulo: She's okay. Sometimes we work well together, but (other / others) days I don't understand her management style.

6. Flight attendant 1: Your flight was crowded and late arriving to Buenos Aires. How were the passengers?

   Flight attendant 2: Some passengers were calm, (other / others) were angry, and (other / others) were confused.

7. Volunteer 1: Where have all the donations come from?

   Volunteer 2: Some have come from religious organizations, (other / others) donations have come from schools, and still (other / others) have come from individual people.

12 Practice

Complete the sentences with *the other, the others,* or *another.*

1. Mitch is taking five classes. Two are interesting, but ____________ aren't.
2. Our team needs ____________ week to finish the project.
3. Duane ate one hamburger, then he ate ____________, and ____________, and ____________!
4. Denise has two neighbors. One is friendly, but ____________ isn't.
5. We need ____________ $6,000 to finish the house.
6. The company interviewed eight candidates for the positions. Four of them were overqualified, three didn't have the skills we need, but ____________ was perfect for the job.
7. Patricia knew some of the students but not ____________.
8. The violinist has released a record a year for the last six years. We have two of them but not ____________.

13 Practice

Answer the questions.

1. Underline every other letter. A B C D E F G H I
2. What's every other day of the week? Sunday, ____________
3. Underline every other year. 1998, 1999, 2000, 2001, 2002, 2003, 2004, 2005, 2006
4. What's every other month in the year? ____________

14 Practice

Read these sentences. Write *C* next to the sentence if *the other, the others, other, others, every other,* or *another* is used correctly. Write *I* if it is used incorrectly.

______ **1.** We'll be there in the other half an hour.

______ **2.** The players don't get along with each other.

______ **3.** Cost is one reason I can't go to Australia, but there are the others.

______ **4.** Lydia works out every other day.

______ **5.** My mom is one of my heroes, but I have many anothers.

______ **6.** One foot is bigger than the other.

______ **7.** Only 50 guests came to the reception. Some never got their invitations, and others got them late.

______ **8.** Go to bed right now. I don't want to hear another excuse.

5d The Indefinite Articles *A* and *An*; *One* and *Ones*

Student Book p. 134

15 Practice

Read these sentences. Write *C* next to the sentence if the article is used correctly. Write *I* if it is used incorrectly.

______ **1.** What time is it? I don't have watch.

______ **2.** Did we have an assignment for tomorrow?

______ **3.** Does anyone have a cell phone?

______ **4.** I need to make call.

______ **5.** All living things need an air to breathe.

______ **6.** Grapes cost $0.69 a pound.

______ **7.** Bill works out three days week.

______ **8.** Jessie needs a new wallet.

______ **9.** Before the sales department makes decision, they need more information.

______ **10.** I like to have an apple for breakfast in the morning.

16 Practice

Read the paragraph about Joel. Complete the sentences with *a, an,* or *one.*

My nephew, Joel, hasn't had ______(1) job in over ______(2) year. He got ______(3) call today telling him that he has ______(4) interview on Thursday. Joel needs ______(5) haircut, ______(6) new suit, ______(7) better résumé, and he only has ______(8) reference. His interview is at 9:00 in the morning, but I'm not sure he has ______(9) alarm clock. I hope ______(10) day, he'll be more organized!

17 Practice

Rewrite the sentences replacing the repeated nouns with *one* or *ones*. You may need to make other changes to the articles in the sentences.

1. Sharlene: Don, do you want a soda?

Don: No, thanks. I already have a soda. *No, thanks. I already have one*.

2. My teacher likes the old designs better than the new designs.

______.

3. Vanessa: What's on TV tonight?

Tom: I don't know. I don't have a TV.

______.

4. Sean: Which car did she get?

Vicky: She got the red car.

______.

5. My inbox was filled with messages, so I deleted the old messages.

______.

6. Rosa: How was the conference?

Sadiq: It was the worst conference I've ever been to!

______________________________.

7. Allen: Oh, no! My computer has crashed!

Tyra: Use the computer at the library.

______________________________.

8. Enrique: How are you doing in your history class?

Tim: Okay. I failed the first test, but passed the other tests.

______________________________.

9. Salesperson: The earrings on the counter are full price, but the earrings in the basket are on sale. ______________________________

______________________________.

18 Practice

Think about your future. Start your sentences with "one day."

1. *One day, I'm going to have a house with a pool*.
2. ______________________________.
3. ______________________________.
4. ______________________________.
5. ______________________________.

5e The Definite Article *The*

Student Book p. 139

19 Practice

Add *the* to the sentences if necessary. If it's not necessary, don't add anything.

1. Everyone should drink __________ water.
2. __________ water in our city doesn't taste very good.
3. Frank went to __________ store.
4. I got some fruit. Please put __________ bananas on the counter.

5. Ben and his friends are planning a trip to __________________ Europe.

6. Look at __________________ stars! They're beautiful tonight.

7. Neil Armstrong was _______________ first person to walk on _______________ moon.

8. My sister's family has a rabbit, a cat, and a dog. __________________ rabbit and _______________ dog get along well, but _______________ cat doesn't like anyone!

9. Manuel loves __________________ animals.

10. __________________ animals on our rescue farm get good care.

20 Practice

Read the article about surfing. Cross out *the* whenever it's not necessary.

The [1] surfing originated in the [2] Hawaiian Islands. The [3] first European to record a description of it was the [4] Lieutenant James King. The [5] surfing is called "The [6] Sport of Kings." Hawaiian royalty had beaches and surfboards that were different from everyone else's. Hawaiian culture had strict rules, but as more and more the [7] Westerners came to Hawaii, the [8] traditions and culture changed. The [9] surfing on the [10] Hawaii fell off, but never died out completely. In the [11] 1850s, surfing began to gain in popularity again.

21 Practice

Complete the sentences with your own ideas.

1. **a.** Japanese is ___fun to study___.

   b. The Japanese are ___very polite___.

2. **a.** People are ______________________________.

   b. The people in my city are ______________________________.

3. **a.** Music is ______________________________.

   b. The music from Jamaica is ______________________________.

4. **a.** Pollution is ______________________________.

   b. The pollution in my city is ______________________________.

5. **a.** Money is ______________________________.

   b. The money in my wallet is ______________________________.

22 Practice

Complete the sentences with *a, an,* or *the.*

1. We're having ___a___ test next week. ___The___ test will cover chapters 6, 7, and 8.
2. I need to get __________ new printer. __________ one I have now is too old.
3. Do you know __________ good babysitter? __________ guy we usually call is busy on Saturday.
4. __________ sun was really hot today! Vince got __________ bad sunburn.
5. Leon has to write __________ book report. I've never heard of __________ book he's chosen.
6. We took __________ taxi yesterday, and I left my sunglasses in __________ cab.
7. Bring __________ sweater with you this weekend. __________ nights can be really cold at our cabin.
8. Rachel had __________ problem with her car. The mechanic says __________ problem is in __________ fuel line.
9. Host: Do you have __________ reservation?

   Guest: Yes, __________ reservation is for 7:00 for four people.

23 Practice

Read the recipe for Easy Fruit Salad. Complete the sentences with *a, an,* or *the.*

Easy Fruit Salad

__________ (1) apple

__________ (2) banana

__________ (3) orange

a few grapes

__________ (4) melon*

(* or any other fruit you like)

__________ (5) lemon

2 Tablespoons of honey or any kind of jam

To make the sauce, squeeze __________ (6) lemon into __________ (7) medium-size bowl. Add __________ (8) honey and mix well.

To make the fruit salad, cut up __________ (9) apple, __________ (10) melon, and __________ (11) banana into __________ (12) bowl. Peel __________ (13) orange and add it and __________ (14) grapes into __________ (15) fruit mixture. Fold __________ (16) fruit and sauce gently together and serve!

24 Practice

Write a recipe for something you like to make.
Write a list of ingredients and instructions.

____

____

____

____

____

____

SELF-TEST

A Choose the best answer, A, B, C, or D, to complete the sentence. Mark your answer by darkening the oval with the same letter.

1. Everyone has to do _____ own work.

A. they (A) (B) (C) (D)
B. their
C. our
D. my

2. My family drives me crazy, but I love _____ all.

A. them (A) (B) (C) (D)
B. theirs
C. it
D. we

3. In order to win the contest, you must complete the task by _____.

A. myself (A) (B) (C) (D)
B. yourself
C. himself
D. itself

4. The children made the dinner by _____.

A. ourselves (A) (B) (C) (D)
B. yourselves
C. themselves
D. herself

5. Al and Matt saw a couple of movies this weekend. One was terrible, but _____ was pretty good.

A. each other (A) (B) (C) (D)
B. another
C. the other
D. other

6. Lisa needs to get _____ job. The one she has now doesn't pay enough.

A. each other (A) (B) (C) (D)
B. another
C. the other
D. other

7. Naoko's family goes to _____ Netherlands every other year.

A. an (A) (B) (C) (D)
B. a
C. one
D. the

8. I've got _____ headache.

A. an (A) (B) (C) (D)
B. a
C. one
D. the

9. _____ speak Korean.

A. They Koreans (A) (B) (C) (D)
B. The Koreans
C. The Koreans people
D. The people

10. The family took a trip around _____ world.

A. an (A) (B) (C) (D)
B. a
C. one
D. the

B Find the underlined word or phrase, A, B, C, or D, that is incorrect. Mark your answer by darkening the oval with the same letter.

1. She's a (A) very skilled manager. She worked hers (B) way up by herself (C). I model my career on hers (D) because she's so successful.

Ⓐ Ⓑ Ⓒ Ⓓ

2. Please, help ourselves (A). There's plenty of food for everyone (B). Ursula made her (C) famous cookies. They're (D) delicious.

Ⓐ Ⓑ Ⓒ Ⓓ

3. Let's have the other (A) party soon! Everyone had a good time. The guests helped themselves (B) to food and introduced themselves (C) to each other (D).

Ⓐ Ⓑ Ⓒ Ⓓ

4. This was a (A) great party! The kids behaved themselves (B) and we enjoyed yourself (C). Other (D) parties I've been to haven't been much fun.

Ⓐ Ⓑ Ⓒ Ⓓ

5. I gave herself (A) a (B) headache thinking about it. It's too difficult to solve by myself (C). I need help from the others (D) on our team.

Ⓐ Ⓑ Ⓒ Ⓓ

6. Can you get me another (A) knife? This one (B) is dirty. Steve will be late for the (C) dinner party, but each other (D) will be on time.

Ⓐ Ⓑ Ⓒ Ⓓ

7. Jack Campbell bought a (A) tent, a (B) sleeping bag, the (C) ice chest, and a (D) backpack for his camping trip.

Ⓐ Ⓑ Ⓒ Ⓓ

8. People speak the Portuguese (A) in Brazil, English (B) in Australia, French (C) in France, and Japanese (D) in Japan.

Ⓐ Ⓑ Ⓒ Ⓓ

9. Linda has to have the (A) best clothes, a (B) most expensive jewelry, the (C) biggest car, and the (D) nicest house.

Ⓐ Ⓑ Ⓒ Ⓓ

10. Michael can play the (A) guitar, the (B) piano, one (C) harmonica, and the flute (D).

Ⓐ Ⓑ Ⓒ Ⓓ

UNIT 6 MODALS I

6b *Can, Could,* and *Be Able To* to Express Ability

Student Book p. 153

1 Practice

Complete the sentences with *can, could,* or *be able to* in the correct tense. More than one answer may be possible.

1. Karen: Why didn't you go?
   Jim: I (not) __________________ find anyone to take my class.
2. Police officer: How did you escape from the locked room?
   Vince: I __________________ reach the window, open it a little, and yell for help.
3. Boss: __________________ (you) stay late tomorrow?
   Assistant: No, I'm sorry. I (not) __________________ stay late.
4. Mark: Darla __________________ always get reservations at the best sushi restaurant in town.
   Jeff: She's lucky. Whenever I call, I (not) __________________ get a reservation for the day I want.
5. The director __________________ see you tomorrow at 10:30 A.M.
6. Seth: How (you) __________________ reach the top shelf?
   Anita: I __________________ reach the top shelf by standing on a dining room chair.
7. We __________________ (not) get cheap tickets, so we're not going to Europe this summer.
8. Jay __________________ do back flips off the diving board when he was 12 years old, but he (not) __________________ now.
9. Andrea __________________ get another ticket for the fashion show next week, so we __________________ all go together.
10. Last week, I __________________ buy a bunch of books on sale!

2 Practice

Answer the questions with your own ideas. Write complete sentences in the tenses given.

1. Can you write html code?

   ____.

2. Are you able to wiggle your ears?

   ____.

3. Could you whistle using your fingers when you were a child?

   ____.

4. Are you able to touch your nose with your tongue?

   ____.

5. Could you do magic tricks when you were younger?

   ____.

6. Can't you flip your eyelids inside out?

   ____.

7. Weren't you able to curl your tongue?

   ____.

8. Will you be able to walk on your hands if you practice?

   ____.

9. Won't you be able to change a flat tire if I show you how?

   ____.

10. Couldn't you run fast as a child?

    ____.

3 Practice

Answer the questions using *can* or *be able to* and your own ideas.

1. The cat's up our tree. How can we get him down?

   You can wait for him to get down by himself. You can call the fire department. You can climb up after him.

2. How can you get in your apartment when you lock your keys inside?

____.

3. How will you be able to start your car if the battery is dead?

____.

4. How can you call someone if you don't have their number?

____.

5. How can you travel globally with very little money?

____.

6. How can you decorate your apartment without spending a lot of money?

____.

* **Bonus:** In one room there are three light switches. In another room there are three lights. How can you determine which switch turns on which light by going into each room only one time?
Note: There are no holes in the walls, special tools, mirrors, equipment, or other people to help you.

4 Practice

Read the paragraph on the Mayans and their accomplishments. Write sentences about them with *could* or *were able to*. More than one answer may be possible.

The Mayans, a group of ancient people that lived in modern day Mexico, Belize, Guatemala, and Honduras, existed from about 2000 B.C. to A.D. 1500. At the peak of their civilization, they were builders, artists, astronomers, farmers, and mathematicians. They predicted eclipses, studied the planets and constellations, and understood the lunar cycle. They built cities, observatories, palaces, ball fields, reservoirs for water storage, and temples, all without metal tools! They cleared the jungle to make farmland and grew cotton, corn, beans, and other vegetables. They developed three calendar systems, including one that has a 360-day year, and used a writing system which combined pictographs and sound characters.

1. *The Mayans could/were able to tell time*.
2. ____.
3. ____.
4. ____.

5. ____.

6. ____.

7. ____.

6c *Must, Have To,* and *Have Got To* to Express Obligation and Necessity

Student Book p. 156

5 Practice

Read the rules about driving. Match the verbs on the left with the ideas on the right. Then write sentences using *have to* or *must*.

__e__	**1.** stop completely	**a.** when you back up
_____	**2.** change oil	**b.** to change gears
_____	**3.** step on clutch	**c.** at all times
_____	**4.** turn headlights on	**d.** every 2,500 miles
_____	**5.** get insurance	**e.** at red lights
_____	**6.** signal	**f.** when driving at night
_____	**7.** wear seatbelts	**g.** when you buy a car
_____	**8.** look behind you	**h.** before you turn

1. *You must stop completely at red lights*.

2. ____.

3. ____.

4. ____.

5. ____.

6. ____.

7. ____.

8. ____.

Bonus Answer: Turn on one switch and let it stay on for an hour or so. Turn it off and flip a different switch. Go into the room with the lights. Find the light that's hot—that one is connected to the first switch. The light that's on goes to the second switch, and the cool light that is off goes with the third switch.

6 Practice

Kate and Pedro are talking about rules in the woodworking class. Complete the sentences with *must, have got to,* or the correct tense of *have to.* More than one answer may be possible.

Kate: Last year, we ______________ (1) wear our safety glasses all the time.

Pedro: That's Mr. Thompson's strictest rule this year, too. We ______________ (2) wear them all the time.

Kate: What's the rule about equipment? When I took the class, we ______________ (3) return equipment at the end of each week.

Pedro: We ______________ (4) return equipment after two days, but next year, we ______________ (5) return equipment the same day it's checked out.

Kate: Yeah, I've heard the accident rule is changing next year, too. Last year, we ______________ (6) report all accidents within a week. Next year, we ______________ (7) report them immediately.

Pedro: At least some rules are staying the same! This year in class, each person ______________ (8) keep their work area clean, and next year each person ______________ (9) keep their work area clean, too.

Kate: That makes sense. I ______________ (10) keep my area clean when I took the class.

Pedro: It's all just common sense. We just ______________ (11) follow Mr. Thompson's instructions. He is very clear about that! And students next year ______________ (12) follow even stricter rules—or else!

7 Practice

Read the article about guinea pigs. Then write how to take care of them using *have to, have got to,* or *must.*

Guinea Pigs Make Wonderful Pets!

If you love animals, but have a small apartment, why not get a guinea pig (or two)! Guinea pigs can make wonderful pets. Guinea pigs like company, so think about getting a couple (two females or two males, unless you want lots of baby guinea pigs).

Guinea pigs are affectionate and easy to take care of. They need vitamin C, vegetables, and clean water every day. Guinea pigs like clean cages, so be sure to clean them every three or four days. Newspaper is fine for the bottom of the cage. Guinea pigs are very gentle creatures; so don't make sudden movements or very loud noises near them. They need a safe place to hide and sleep in their cage. Guinea pigs can live ten years, so if you want one, be sure you can make the commitment to take care of him or her for that long.

1. *You have to be ready to take care of one for about ten years before you get one*.
2. ______.
3. ______.
4. ______.
5. ______.
6. ______.

8 Practice

Read the rapid-speech sentences. Write the full forms.

1. "Billy's gotta stop missing so many classes."

   Billy has got to stop missing so many classes.
2. "Sorry, I gotta get going."

   ______.
3. "What did we hafta do?"

   ______.
4. "We hatta empty the trash."

   ______.
5. "Deborah hasta get up at 3:00 A.M. every morning."

   ______.
6. "Yuichiro and Emiko'll hafta study before they'll be able to do anything else!"

   ______.

9 Practice

Write sentences using the correct tense of *have to* or *have got to*. Use the hints and your own ideas.

1. What did you have to do today to get ready for school?

   brush teeth get up

   get dressed shower

   a. I had to get up at 6:00 ______.

   b. ______.

   c. ______.

   d. ______.

2. What will your friends have to do before they will be able to go on vacation?

   arrange for a petsitter make hotel reservations

   book their flights take their exams

   a. ______.

   b. ______.

   c. ______.

   d. ______.

3. What did people have to do 200 years ago?

   candles grow food horses

   a. ______.

   b. ______.

   c. ______.

4. It's the beginning of the school year. What does Lucy have to do to get ready?

   buy textbooks rent an apartment

   find a part-time job set up her computer

   a. ______.

   b. ______.

   c. ______.

   d. ______.

6d *Not Have To* and *Must Not* to Express Prohibition and Lack of Necessity

Student Book p. 159

10 Practice

Mrs. Devine is taking her son to the opera for the first time. Match her instructions on the left with the ideas on the right.

_____	**1.** We don't have to drive.	**a.** A suit is fine.
_____	**2.** You don't have to wear a tuxedo.	**b.** to enjoy the performance.
_____	**3.** You mustn't lose the tickets.	**c.** It's standard policy.
_____	**4.** We mustn't be late	**d.** We're taking a limo.
_____	**5.** You mustn't have your cell phone turned on.	**e.** because we won't be allowed in.
_____	**6.** You don't have to play a musical instrument	**f.** They're irreplaceable.

11 Practice

A father is giving his daughters a lecture about life. Complete the sentences with *have to, not have to,* or *mustn't.*

You ______________ (1) always try to tell the truth. You may not be able to do it all the time, but you ______________ (2) try. You ______________ (3) gossip about others because that hurts them. You ______________ (4) try to control other people either. You ______________ (5) take good care of yourself. You ______________ (6) treat other people the way you want to be treated. You ______________ (7) take on too many projects. You ______________ (8) do for others what they can do for themselves. You ______________ (9) forgive other people because it only hurts you if you don't. You ______________ (10) try to make the world a better place.

What are some rules that you live by? Use *have to* or *mustn't* in your answers.

1. ______________________________.
2. ______________________________.
3. ______________________________.

12 Practice

Read the paragraph on photography. Complete the sentences with *have to* or *not have to* in the correct verb tense.

When photography was invented, photographers ______ (1) hold the exposure for several minutes to get a clear image. Now, of course, people ______ (2) use film cameras because digital cameras are very convenient. When you used a film camera, you ______ (3) keep the back of the camera closed until you developed the film. When you bought film, you ______ (4) get the right speed and exposure for the light and conditions. Now, if you don't have a camera, you ______ (5) pay hundreds of dollars for one because there are so many disposable ones on the market. In the future, people ______ (6) use film at all. Photographers ______ (7) carry so much special equipment. In the past, they ______ (8) spend a lot of time developing film in the darkroom. In the future, photographers ______ (9) do that either.

13 Practice

Complete the sentences with your own ideas.

1. Customer service representatives have to _try and help you_, but they don't have to _fix the computer_.
2. Hairstylists have to ____________________, but they don't have to ____________________.
3. A musician has to ____________________, but he or she doesn't have to ____________________.
4. Housekeepers have to ____________________, but they don't have to ____________________.
5. Good friends have to ____________________, but they don't have to ____________________.
6. A gardener has to ____________________, but she or he doesn't have to ____________________.
7. Children have to ____________________, but they don't have to ____________________.
8. A couple has to ____________________, but they don't have to ____________________.

14 Practice

Read the statements. Circle *Agree* or *Disagree* and explain your answer.

1. You don't have to have a college degree to get a good job.

   (Agree) Disagree _If you are passionate about something, you can get a good job without a degree._

2. Teachers mustn't hit students.

   Agree Disagree ____________________

3. Students mustn't sleep in class.

   Agree Disagree ____________________

4. You don't have to have a lot of money to be happy.

   Agree Disagree ____________________

5. Children mustn't talk to strangers.

Agree Disagree ______________________

6. You mustn't make sudden moves around wild animals.

Agree Disagree ______________________

7. People mustn't eat meat.

Agree Disagree ______________________

8. People don't have to get married to have children.

Agree Disagree ______________________

9. You don't have to wrap gifts before you give them.

Agree Disagree ______________________

10. A society doesn't have to have rules.

Agree Disagree ______________________

6e *Should, Ought To,* and *Had Better* to Give Advice

Student Book p. 162

15 Practice

Read the sentences with *had better* and write the possible consequences. Use *or* in your answers.

1. The class had better leave now, or they'll miss the bus.
2. The children had better not eat so much ice cream, ______________________.
3. You'd better be careful working so close to the grill, ______________________.
4. My wife and I'd better stop spending so much money, ______________________.
5. Jin had better start paying more attention in class, ______________________.
6. I think we'd better call a technician, ______________________.
7. The gardener had better water the yard today, ______________________.
8. I'd better get a job soon, ______________________.
9. I'd better work out more, ______________________.
10. I had better ______________________.

16 Practice

Read the following problems. Write suggestions using *should, shouldn't,* or *ought to.*

1. stolen laptop You should call the police and file a report. (OR) You should ask if anyone saw anything.

2. depression

   ______________________.

   ______________________.

3. marital problems

   ______________________.

   ______________________.

4. a bad haircut

   ______________________.

   ______________________.

5. forgetfulness

   ______________________.

   ______________________.

6. high gasoline prices

   ______________________.

   ______________________.

7. insomnia

   ______________________.

   ______________________.

8. dyslexia

   ______________________.

   ______________________.

9. anorexia

   ______________________.

   ______________________.

10. a haunted house

    ______________________.

    ______________________.

17 Practice

Read the dialogues. Think of an appropriate situation for the responses.

1. Ryan: *Ellen just yelled at me in front of everyone at my desk.*
   Hideki: That's terrible!
   Rob: You should talk to her supervisor.

2. Jerome: ______________________________.
   Chandra: That's great!
   Peggy: We should celebrate! Let's call everyone.

3. David: ______________________________.
   Elsie: Well, I understand, but I think you should apologize to her.

4. Beth: ______________________________.
   Ed: Really? You should call the police.

5. Michael: ______________________________.
   Deborah: That's too bad.
   Kevin: You should come to the study sessions. They really help me.

6. Marissa: ______________________________.
   Kyle: That looks terrible! You should put a bandage on that.

7. Gerald: ______________________________.
   Krystal: You did? You should ask for a raise.

18 Practice

Read the questions and give advice using *should (not), ought to,* or *had better.*

1. What should someone do to learn another language?

   ______________________________.

2. What should someone do if he or she is in a car accident?

   ______________________________.

3. What should someone do if their computer crashes?

   ______________________________.

4. What should people do if they have a lot of work to do, but they're too tired to do it?

____.

5. What should someone do to live a better, healthier life?

____.

6f *Should Have* and *Ought To Have* to Express Regret or a Mistake

Student Book p. 164

19 Practice

Read the statements with *should have* and *shouldn't have.* Then write the reality or mistake of each situation.

1. They should have told you when they were going to come back.

   They didn't tell you when they were coming back, and now you feel it was a mistake.

2. I shouldn't have eaten so many cherries. I don't feel very good right now.

   ____.

3. We should have spent more time on our presentation.

   ____.

4. My brother should have returned the library book two days ago.

   ____.

5. You should have introduced yourself to our new neighbors.

   ____.

6. Ugh. I just got off the phone with Angie. I should have let the machine pick it up.

   ____.

7. The homeowners said they shouldn't have left the paint cans so close to the furnace.

   ____.

8. You argue so much that you should have been a lawyer!

   ____.

20 Practice

Kija Lee is a reporter. She's asking people on the street about regrets they have. Read their statements and write their regrets.

A. Kija: Excuse me, sir. Could I ask you a question?

Andy: Sure.

Kija: Do you have any regrets?

Andy: Well, I should have gone to college when I had the chance. But I think it's too late now.

Regret: Andy didn't go to college ______.

And last year I gave my wife a vacuum cleaner for her birthday. I shouldn't have done that!

Regret: ______.

B. Kija: Ma'am. How about you? Do you have any regrets?

Ms. Kim: Well, I should have accepted that job in Vietnam. It was a great opportunity.

Regret: ______.

And I shouldn't have started smoking again. It's so hard to quit!

Regret: ______.

C. Kija: Excuse me, sir. I'm talking with people about regrets. Do you have any that you'd like to share with our readers?

Pierre: I should have checked my parking meter earlier. Look! I got a ticket.

Regret: ______.

No, but seriously. I should have taken my family to the beach for our last vacation. We rented a cabin in the mountains, and it rained every day, and we were without power for most of the time. It was not fun.

Regret: ______________________________.

D. Kija: Excuse me. Do you have any regrets?

You: I should have ______________________________.

Regret: ______________________________.

And I shouldn't have ______________________________.

Regret: ______________________________.

21 Practice

Read the rapid-speech sentences. Write the full forms.

1. "You shoulda been there. It was a riot!"

   You should have been there.

2. "We better get going."

   ______________________________.

3. "Tommy oughta've moved to France."

   ______________________________.

4. "We coulda lent you the money."

   ______________________________.

5. "Kirk musta gotten lost. Otherwise, he woulda been here by now."

   ______________________________.

6. "Do we hafta do this right now?"

   ______________________________.

7. "Who shoulda done this?"

   ______________________________.

8. "Spock always hasta solve the problems on the ship."

   ______________________________.

22 Practice

Read the situations and complete the sentences. Use the words in parentheses and your own ideas. Be sure to use *not* if you write a negative sentence.

1. Yesterday the electric company was working on the utility pole outside my house. This morning when I looked outside, the pole was on fire! Luckily, the fire department came quickly and put out the fire.

   a. The crew (must) *must have done something wrong yesterday*.

   (OR) *They must not have fixed it*.

   b. The fire (could) *could have spread to other houses*.

   c. The crew (should) *should have made sure their work was finished yesterday*.

2. A young couple moved into the apartment next to me last month. Today I saw the woman packing boxes and carrying suitcases to her car. I haven't seen the man in a while.

   a. They (may) ______.

   b. She (must) ______.

   c. They (should) ______.

3. At Maureen's favorite seafood restaurant yesterday, she tried crab for the first time. She usually has shrimp, but she wanted to try something different. An hour after lunch, Maureen got sick.

   a. She (must) ______.

   b. She (could) ______.

   c. She (should) ______.

4. Zoe is a software consultant. She bills her customers every month. Last month she changed her accounting software, and she hasn't received any checks yet this month.

   a. She (must) ______.

   b. She (should) ______.

   c. She (could) ______.

23 Practice

Answer the questions. Write sentences with *should have* or *shouldn't have.*

1. In your opinion, what is a mistake or decision that your government has made that you disagree with. What should (not) they have done?

   ____

   ____________________.

2. What is a mistake or decision that your best friend has made that you disagree with? What should (not) he or she have done?

   ____

   ____________________.

3. What is a mistake or decision that your parents have made that you disagree with? What should (not) they have done?

   ____

   ____________________.

6g *Be Supposed To* to Express Expectation

Student Book p. 167

24 Practice

Rachel and Yuri are teaching their children table manners. Write sentences with *be supposed to* or *not be supposed to* and the following ideas.

1. put elbows on the table

   You're not supposed to put your elbows on the table.

2. wait until everyone is seated before starting to eat

   ____________________.

3. chew with your mouth open

   ____________________.

4. say you don't like something

   ____________________.

   leave it on your plate

   ____________________.

5. put your napkin in your lap

____.

6. cover your mouth and say "excuse me" if you burp

____.

7. reach across the table to get something you want

____.

ask someone politely to pass it to you

____.

What are some other manners that children are taught?

1. ____.
2. ____.
3. ____.

25 Practice

Read the sentences about Holly and Steve meeting friends at a concert. Write possible ideas for why their plans went wrong. Answer the questions.

1. We were supposed to meet Betty and Mike at 7:00, *but we never met them*.
2. We were supposed to leave our house at 6:00, but ______________________________.
3. They were supposed to call one of us on our cell phones if we missed each other, but ______________________________.
4. We were supposed to have dinner with them, but ______________________________.
5. There were supposed to be fireworks after the concert, but ______________________________.
6. It wasn't supposed to rain, but ______________________________.

Read the statements. Fill in *T* if the statement is true and *F* if the statement is false.

1. Holly and Steve met Betty and Mike at the concert. (T) (F)
2. Holly and Steve didn't leave their house at 6:00. (T) (F)
3. They all ate dinner together. (T) (F)
4. There were fireworks. (T) (F)
5. It didn't rain. (T) (F)

SELF-TEST

A Choose the best answer, A, B, C, or D, to complete the sentence. Mark your answer by darkening the oval with the same letter.

1. The Browns _____ go camping with us.

A. might could
B. may be able to
C. can to
D. didn't could

Ⓐ Ⓑ Ⓒ Ⓓ

2. Jake _____ move the sofa. He found his keys on the bed.

A. didn't must to
B. must to
C. have to
D. didn't have to

Ⓐ Ⓑ Ⓒ Ⓓ

3. The firm _____ better sign the contract tomorrow, or they'll miss the opportunity.

A. had
B. have
C. ought to
D. should

Ⓐ Ⓑ Ⓒ Ⓓ

4. The new law says that drivers _____ block the sidewalk.

A. must not
B. don't must
C. should to
D. ought to

Ⓐ Ⓑ Ⓒ Ⓓ

5. Theresa _____ returned the phone call, but she didn't get the message until this morning.

A. had to
B. should
C. should have
D. was able to

Ⓐ Ⓑ Ⓒ Ⓓ

6. The women _____ to meet their trainer at 6:30 A.M.

A. must
B. are supposed
C. should
D. had better

Ⓐ Ⓑ Ⓒ Ⓓ

7. You _____ told her your opinion. She didn't ask you for it.

A. didn't have to
B. should
C. could
D. shouldn't have

Ⓐ Ⓑ Ⓒ Ⓓ

8. I think we _____ better compare prices before we decide which DVD player to get.

A. should
B. could
C. had
D. must

Ⓐ Ⓑ Ⓒ Ⓓ

9. Miriam _____ turn down the oven, but she turned it up instead. Now the pie is burned.

A. is supposed to
B. was able to
C. was supposed to
D. had better to

Ⓐ Ⓑ Ⓒ Ⓓ

10. Helen _____ email me back, but she did.

A. mustn't
B. didn't have to
C. had to
D. supposed to

Ⓐ Ⓑ Ⓒ Ⓓ

B Find the underlined word or phrase, A, B, C, or D, that is incorrect. Mark your answer by darkening the oval with the same letter.

1. Frankie has (A) finish the paper tonight because he won't be (B) able (C) to (D) tomorrow.

   Ⓐ Ⓑ Ⓒ Ⓓ

2. Karl should (A) have (B) read (C) the directions before he started playing the game. He better (D) take a look at them now.

   Ⓐ Ⓑ Ⓒ Ⓓ

3. Jay shouldn't have (A) accepted the position. He can't (B) the job. He's (C) supposed (D) to tell them tomorrow that he quits.

   Ⓐ Ⓑ Ⓒ Ⓓ

4. I'll have to (A) check (B) my calendar, but we may (C) able to go (D) with you.

   Ⓐ Ⓑ Ⓒ Ⓓ

5. Someone is (A) supposed come (B) tomorrow to look for the leak. I couldn't (C) climb up there, so I can't (D) fix it.

   Ⓐ Ⓑ Ⓒ Ⓓ

6. You should (A) called the architect before we left. She was (B) supposed to (C) have the plans ready but she doesn't. Now what are we supposed to (D) do?

   Ⓐ Ⓑ Ⓒ Ⓓ

7. Sue and I ought to (A) have (B) went (C) to the gym, but we couldn't (D) wake up this morning.

   Ⓐ Ⓑ Ⓒ Ⓓ

8. High school students must (A) wear uniforms. Girls mustn't (B) wear (C) short skirts, and boys don't must (D) wear jeans.

   Ⓐ Ⓑ Ⓒ Ⓓ

9. You're supposed (A) to offer your seat to the elderly. You don't had to (B), but you (C) should (D).

   Ⓐ Ⓑ Ⓒ Ⓓ

10. I can drive (A) here because I have a driver's license. Yesterday, I could (B) rent a car. I was (C) able to (D) get a good price on it, too.

   Ⓐ Ⓑ Ⓒ Ⓓ

UNIT 7 MODALS II

7a *Shall, Let's, How About, What About, Why Don't, Could,* and *Can* to Make Suggestions

Student Book p. 180

1 Practice

Edna and Lucy are looking for somewhere to have lunch. Complete the sentences with *how about, what about, shall, could,* or *can*. More than one answer may be possible.

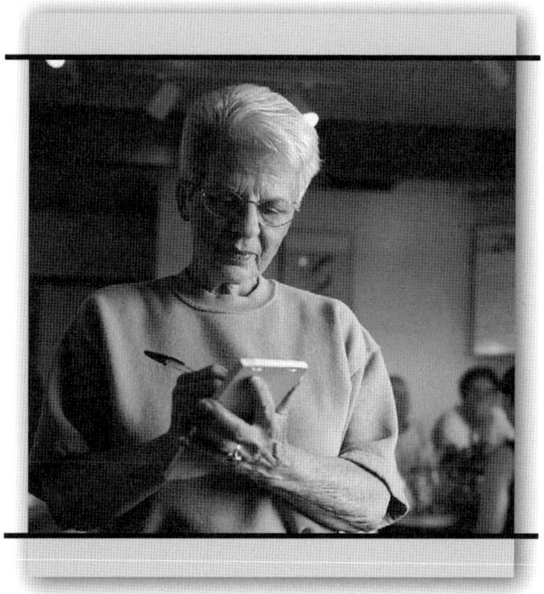

Edna: This place looks interesting.

__________ (1) we have lunch here?

Lucy: Okay. __________ (2) just having a light lunch? Then we __________ (3) go for a run later.

Edna: All right. That's a good idea.

They go into the restaurant.

Edna: __________ (4) we sit by the window?

Lucy: Definitely. That's a nice view of the bay.

Edna (*to server*): Hello. __________ (5) sitting near the window? Is that possible?

Server: Yes, of course.

Edna: Hmm. I don't know what to order.

Server: Well, __________ (6) trying the special? It's chicken salad, and it has chicken, raisins, and walnuts in it.

Edna: I'm allergic to walnuts. Maybe the chef __________ (7) leave them out.

Server: I'm sorry. It's already made. __________ (8) the penne with spring vegetables? It comes with salad and garlic bread.

Edna: That sounds perfect.

Lucy: I'd like the same thing, but I don't really like garlic bread.

Server: I __________ (9) ask the chef to give you plain bread instead.

Lucy: Thanks. I'd appreciate that.

Server: ______(10)______ something to drink?

Edna: I'll have iced tea, please.

Lucy: Just water for me, thanks.

2 Practice

Read the dialogue between two college roommates. Complete the sentences with *let's, how about, what about, could,* or *can*. More than one answer may be possible.

Michele: We have two hours before class. What do you want to do?

Natalie: *How about/What about* (1) going home and taking a nap?

Michele: I don't want to do that. ______(2)______ do some shopping. We ______(3)______ check out that new shoe store on Pine.

Natalie: Or, we ______(4)______ go to the library and take a nap.

Michele: Natalie! I don't want to take a nap!

Natalie: Okay, okay. ______(5)______ getting some coffee then? I'm really sleepy.

Michele: Okay. There's a coffee shop next to the shoe store. ______(6)______ go there first.

3 Practice

The phrases of suggestion in the following sentences are incorrect. Rewrite the sentences correctly three different ways using *how about, let's,* and *why don't*. Add question marks if necessary.

1. How about turn on some music.

How about turning on some music? **(OR)**

Let's turn on some music. **(OR)**

Why don't we/you turn on some music?

2. Why don't order a pizza.

____

____

____

3. Let's us meet at my house.

4. Let's not taking the highway.

5. Why don't taking my car.

6. How about we going now.

7. Why we don't take some more time before we decide.

8. Let's we go to the lake this weekend. It's going to be beautiful.

9. How about not play card games for a change.

10. Let's going out for dinner.

____

____

____

4 Practice

A friend doesn't know what to do with his/her future. Write suggestions using *how about, what about, could,* and *why don't.*

You could take classes to find out what you're interested in.

Why don't you make an appointment with a career counselor?

____

____

7b *Prefer, Would Prefer,* and *Would Rather* to Express Preferences

Student Book p. 182

5 Practice

Complete the sentences with *prefer* or *would rather* and *to* or *than* if necessary.

Laura: I'm thinking about planting vegetables in our garden. What do you think?

Kevin: Really? I ________ (1) have a flower garden.

Laura: But we live so far away from the grocery store, I ________ (2) grow my own tomatoes ________ (3) go eight miles. I also ________ (4) the flavor of fresh vegetables ________ (5) store bought ones.

Kevin: Yes, but a vegetable garden takes more time than a flower garden. When I get home from work, I ________ (6) relaxing ________ (7) watering and weeding the garden.

Laura: You won't have to do anything. I ________ (8) take care of it myself anyway.

6 Practice

Complete the sentences on the left with the endings on the right.

______	**1.** The children prefer water	**a.**	than go to the movies.
______	**2.** Jessica would rather stay home	**b.**	to eating out.
______	**3.** The royal family would prefer	**c.**	rather eat tofu than seafood.
______	**4.** Josh prefers cooking at home	**d.**	to juice.
______	**5.** Samantha would	**e.**	not to comment on the situation.

7 Practice

Answer the questions with your own ideas. Explain your preferences.

1. Do you prefer to drive or take taxis?

*I prefer to take taxis. I don't like driving*______________.

2. Would you rather spend money flying in first class or have the extra money to spend on your vacation?

____.

3. Would you rather work for someone else or be your own boss?

____.

4. Do you prefer spicy food to mild food?

____.

5. When you go out, would you rather listen to a DJ or listen to a live band?

____.

6. When you eat dinner, would you rather sit at a table or eat in front of the TV?

____.

7. Do you prefer to work out at the gym or to go for a run outside?

____.

8. Do you prefer eating at fast-food restaurants to eating at home?

____.

8 Practice

Write as many questions and answers as you can using *would rather* and *prefer* and the following ideas.

1. history / physics

- **Q:** Would you rather study history or physics?

  A: I'd rather study physics than (study) history.
- **Q:** Do you prefer history to physics?

  A: No, I prefer physics (to history).
- **Q:** Do you prefer studying history to studying physics?

  A: No, I prefer studying physics (to studying history).
- **Q:** Do you prefer to study history?

  A: No, I don't.

2. work with numbers / work with people

3. drive a car / ride a motorcycle

4. gardening / reading

5. talk about your problems with other people / solve them by yourself

____

____

____

____

7c *May, Could,* and *Can* to Ask Permission

Student Book p. 186

9 Practice

Complete the sentences with *may, could,* or *can*. More than one answer may be possible.

A. James: Excuse me. ________ (1) I take a train schedule?

Clerk: Yes, you ________ (2). Anything else?

James: Yes, ________ (3) I also take the list of fares?

Clerk: No, I'm afraid you ________ (4) because there isn't a complete list. However, you ________ (5) take anything on the counter.

B. Danielle is talking to her best friend.

Danielle: Claudia? It's me. ________ (1) I talk to you for a minute?

Claudia: Yes, but I ________ (2) talk for very long. What's up?

Danielle: I need a favor. ________ (3) I use your bike tomorrow?

Claudia: Sure, you ________ (4). Why?

Danielle: Mine has a flat tire, and I need to go by the post office.

Claudia: No problem. You ________ (5) borrow it anytime you need to.

C. Sue: Sean, ________ (1) my sister stay at your apartment for a few days while you are out of town next week? She's in town interviewing.

Sean: That's fine. She ________ (2) stay there the whole week if she needs to.

Sue: ________ (3) she give your number to people while she's there?

Sean: Yes, she ________ (4), but she ________ (5) give it to just anyone!

D. Helga: ________ (1) I smoke in here?

Host: Sorry, you ________ (2). But you ________ (3) smoke out on the patio.

10 Practice

Write *a* or *b* beside each sentence to identify if the modal is used to talk about ability or permission.

______ **1.** You may be excused.	**a.** ability
______ **2.** Could I look at your notes?	**b.** permission
______ **3.** Beverly could speak Italian fluently when she was in 6th grade.	
______ **4.** May I speak with you for a few minutes?	
______ **5.** You can have my sandwich. I'm not hungry.	
______ **6.** Cats can see in the dark.	
______ **7.** We can see our house from here!	
______ **8.** Could we sit near the front?	
______ **9.** Dad said we could go with you.	
______ **10.** Phil could easily run a 10K when he was younger.	

11 Practice

Use the prompts to write dialogues with *may, could,* or *can*. More than one modal may be correct.

1. You want to miss class. Ask your teacher. He gives you permission.

You: Mr. Faber, may I be absent tomorrow? My parents are coming for a visit.

Mr. Faber: Sure. That's no problem. Just ask someone about the homework.

2. You want to study in the United States. Ask your parents. They give you permission.

____?

____.

3. Your boss wants you to work late. You have a dentist's appointment at 6:00.

____?

____.

4. Your best friend wants to borrow your digital camera. The camera is broken.

____?

____.

5. You want to see the dessert menu. Ask the server. He says "yes."

____?

____.

6. Your favorite movie star is sitting at a restaurant. Ask her for an autograph. She says "yes."

____?

____.

7. You want to try on a different pair of shoes. Ask the shoe salesperson. He says "yes."

____?

____.

7d *Will, Can, Could, Would,* and *Would You Mind* to Make Requests

Student Book p. 190

12 Practice

Read some common questions travelers ask in an English-speaking country. Complete the sentences with *could, would,* or *would you mind.*

1. ______________ you tell me how to get to Sutter Street, please?
2. ______________ you repeat that? I didn't hear what you said.
3. ______________ repeating that?
4. ______________ you tell me where the hotel is?
5. ______________ you tell me if you have a vacancy, please?
6. ______________ telling me where the nearest restaurant is?
7. ______________ taking our photo, please?
8. ______________ you take our photo, please?
9. ______________ hailing a cab for me, please?

13 Practice

Jack is asking his friends to help him move. What do their responses mean? Write *accept* or *decline* next to each answer.

Jack: Hey, guys. Would you guys mind helping me move on Saturday?

1. ___decline___ Walter: No way!
2. ________ Bob: Sure.
3. ________ Sanjay: Sorry.
4. ________ Kenneth: Yeah, okay.
5. ________ Sung Hee: I can't.
6. ________ Erik: No, I'd be happy to.
7. ________ Jerry: Yes, I'll be out of town.

How many people are going to help him move? ________

14 Practice

There are mistakes in the following sentences. Cross out incorrect words and add other words as necessary to correct them.

1. Would you mind ~~turn~~ turning down the music?
2. Would you going shopping with me?
3. **A:** Could you work late tonight?

   B: Yes, I could.
4. **A:** Would you picking up some butter?

   B: Sure.
5. Would you mind come with me?
6. **A:** Could you lend me your MP3 player?

   B: No, I couldn't. Sorry.
7. **A:** Would you mind not park there?

   B: Oh, sorry!
8. **A:** Would you helping me with this exercise?

   B: No problem.

15 Practice

Write requests based on the following information.

1. A friend of yours plays guitar. You would like to learn. Ask him/her.

   Could you teach me how to play guitar?

2. You need a ride to work because your car isn't working. Ask a coworker.

   ____

3. You still don't understand the unit. Ask your teacher to postpone the test.

   ____

4. The phone's ringing. You have just gotten out of the shower. Ask your roommate to answer it.

   ____

5. You and your roommate share housework, but he/she hasn't washed his/her dishes in a week. Ask them to.

   ____

6. Your girlfriend/boyfriend always talks during movies. Ask him/her to be quiet.

   ____

7. You need a new pair of glasses. The designer frames you really like cost $500. Ask a friend to loan you some money.

   ____

8. You're going to a party and your roommate has a new sweater that would look GREAT on you. Ask him/her to borrow it.

   ____

9. You are at a café and you need to use the restroom. Ask the clerk for the key.

   ____

7e *May, Might,* and *Could* to Express Possibility

Student Book p. 194

16 Practice

Write *a* or *b* beside each sentence to identify if the modal is used to talk about something that is/was possible or something that is/was impossible.

a. possible
b. impossible

_____ **1.** I couldn't have gone with you. I had to work.

_____ **2.** You drove? Jin could have gone with you.

_____ **3.** We may need to get gas soon.

_____ **4.** He may have called, and we didn't hear the phone.

_____ **5.** Joon Hee might take some online classes this summer.

_____ **6.** The Leiers could have seen Notre Dame but they went to Versailles instead.

_____ **7.** I couldn't have done it without your help.

_____ **8.** Dr. O'Malley couldn't have driven this morning. His car's still in the driveway.

_____ **9.** The sales team may finish their work by midnight if everything goes okay.

_____ **10.** Sarah thinks she might get an "A" on her next test.

17 Practice

Read the conversations. Answer the questions with *may, might,* or *could* to express possibility in the present.

1. Ana: What has happened to your computer?

Luke: I'm not sure. *It might have a virus.* (OR) *The server could be busy.*

Ana: What are you going to do if it doesn't work?

Luke: ______________________________.

Ana: How are you going to finish the report?

Luke: I don't know. ______________________________.

2. A: Wow. This is a really good salad. What's in it? What do you think?

B: I don't know. ______________________________ or

______________________________.

3: A: How are you going to decorate your new home?

B: I'm not sure, yet. ______________________________ in the living room,

but ______________________________ in the bedrooms.

And ______________________________ in the kitchen.

A: How about the back yard?

B: That's a problem. It's so big. ______________________________.

4. A: How does that magician float in air?!

B: I don't really know, but ______________________________.

5. A: I dreamt I was walking through a green room, and when I looked out the window, I saw my best friend sitting in a tree waving at me. What do you think it means?

B: I have no idea, but ______________________________ or

______________________________.

18 Practice

Answer the questions in two ways. Use *may, might,* or *could* + *have* + a past participle to express possibility in the past.

1. A: Why didn't Paige call you back last night?

B: _She might not have had time_. (OR) _She could have been too busy last night_.

2. A: Why didn't our English teacher assign any homework yesterday?

B: ______________________________.

______________________________.

3. A: What has happened to Michael? He looks terrible.

B: I don't know. ______________________________.

______________________________.

4. A: Do you know why Pedro quit his job last week?

B: ______________________________.

______________________________.

5. **A:** Why did Karina start smoking again last summer?

B: ____.

____.

6. **A:** Why didn't Nikki introduce herself to you at the party?

B: ____.

____.

7. **A:** Whoa! Did you see that? I wonder why that car ran the red light!

B: ____.

____.

8. **A:** Have you seen Cheryl? Why has she cut her hair so short?

B: ____.

____.

19 Practice

Read the questions. Answer them with your own ideas. Use *may, might,* or *could* + *have* + a past participle to express possibility in the past.

1. How was Stonehenge built? Who built it?

   It could have been built by druids or ancient priests.

   It might have been built by aliens (just kidding!).

2. How did the dinosaurs become extinct?

   ____

   ____

3. How was the universe created?

   ____

   ____

Think of some other mysteries. Write possible explanations for them.

4. ____

   ____

5. ______________________________

____

6. ______________________________

____

7f *Should* and *Ought To* to Express Probability

Student Book p. 198

20 Practice

Complete the sentences with the verbs in parentheses. Use *should/ought to* + base verb for things that are probable in the present or future. Use *should/ought to* + *have* + past participle for things that were probable in the past.

1. They're working hard. They (feel) ought to feel/should feel exhausted at the end of their shift.
2. We just ate an hour ago! You (not, be) ______________ hungry yet.
3. I gave the baby some medicine. She (stop) ______________ coughing by now.
4. Roberto is really tired. He (sleep) ______________ well tonight.
5. Lourdes bought the shoes last week. She (try) ______________ them on already.
6. There was no traffic this morning. You (not, be) ______________ late to the meeting.
7. We're going to a four-star restaurant. The food (taste) ______________ superb, and the atmosphere (encourage) ______________ diners to relax.
8. Your car used to be in good condition. You (sell) ______________ it last year.
9. Mr. Potter (return) ______________ soon. He just went to get a cup of coffee.
10. George (not, fail) ______________ the exam. He'd studied most of the weekend!

21 Practice

Complete the sentences about things that have probably happened using the perfect modal form of *should* or *ought to* (*should* or *ought to* + *have*) and the verbs in parentheses.

1. The wedding is in 30 minutes. The flowers (arrive) should have arrived/ ought to have arrived by now.
2. Ann left the job over a month ago. They (post) ______________________ the position.
3. Sam: Your cousin's knee was injured the last time I saw her.
   Bob: Yes, she (have) ______________________ knee surgery, but I haven't heard anything.
4. I mailed the package two weeks ago. You (receive) ______________________ it by this week.
5. Let's go to the mall. It's late. The crowd (die down) ______________________.
6. Lucy and Bill are leaving on the 12th. They (get) ______________________ their tickets by now.
7. Have you heard anything from the police? They (finish) ______________________ the investigation.
8. Barbara is going on a diving trip next week. She (take) ______________________ scuba diving lessons by now.

22 Practice

Read the sentences and use your own ideas to tell why the speaker uses *should* or *ought to* + a base verb or *should/ought to* + *have* + a past participle.

1. The opera is in 10 minutes. The audience ought to be seated by now.

   Normally at an opera, the audience arrives and is seated about 15 minutes before the opera begins. We expect this.

2. The students started the test 90 minutes ago. They should have finished by now.

   ____

   ____.

3. The trip from downtown only takes 40 minutes. They ought to be back any time now.

   ____

   ____.

4. It's 9:30. The mail shouldn't arrive until noon.

   ____

   ____.

5. Let's call Jim. He shouldn't have left yet. It's only 7:30.

   ____

   ____.

6. Today, we should hear if the agent has accepted our offer on the new house.

   ____

   ____.

7. After your massage, you should feel pretty good.

   ____

   ____.

8. We're starting with advanced digital modeling. You should have learned the basics last semester.

   ____

   ____.

7g *Must, Must Not,* and *Can't* to Make Deductions

Student Book p. 200

23 Practice

Write *a* or *b* beside each sentence to identify if *can* or *can't* is used to talk about permission or deduction.

a. permission
b. deduction

_____ **1.** Can I use your computer?

_____ **2.** No, you can't.

_____ **3.** She left five minutes ago. She can't have gone too far.

_____ **4.** My children can only watch five hours of television a week.

_____ **5.** This bill can't be right. The waiter forgot to add on our dessert.

_____ **6.** Everyone can go to the museum today. It's free on Thursdays.

_____ **7.** That clock can't be right. My watch says it's 1:20.

_____ **8.** This coat can't be yours. Yours is on the floor over there.

_____ **9.** Can I adopt a dog, please?

_____ **10.** We can't adopt a dog until we have more time to spend with him or her.

24 Practice

Complete the deductions with *must* or *must not* and the ideas in parentheses.

1. That man is calling for help! He (know how to swim) *must not know how to swim*.

2. Everyone in that family has their own car. They (have a lot of money) ________________.

3. Cindy has two dogs, three cats, and a canary. She (love animals) ________________

____.

4. I'm waving at Sherry, but she's not waving back. She (see us) ________________

____.

5. Toni screamed when she saw the spider. She (be afraid of them) ________________

____.

6. Jennifer's always upbeat. She (worry too much about small issues) ________________

____.

7. Tom and Danny haven't said two words to each other. They (be angry at each other)

____.

8. Franklin never suggests we go to science fiction films. He (enjoy science fiction)

____.

Complete the sentences with your own ideas.

9. This kitchen has everything! The people living here ________________

____.

10. You've finished this exercise already? Modals ________________

____.

25 Practice

Match the sentences on the left with the past deductions on the right.

_____	**1.** Carl is dancing. I can't believe it!	**a.** Something must have happened.
_____	**2.** Oh, no. The dog threw up on the living room carpet.	**b.** The power must have gone off.
_____	**3.** There's an ambulance across the street at the neighbor's.	**c.** She must have eaten something that upset her stomach.
_____	**4.** Kevin got directions off the Internet, but he's not here yet.	**d.** He must have taken lessons.
_____	**5.** My alarm didn't go off, and there are no lights.	**e.** He must not have followed them correctly.

26 Practice

Read about Armand in high school and now. Write one deduction about the present using *must* and one about the past using *must have* or *must not have.*

In high school	Now
1. Armand weighed 210 pounds.	**1.** Armand weighs 190 pounds.
2. He didn't date anyone in particular.	**2.** He's wearing a wedding ring.
3. He moved to Seattle after graduation.	**3.** He's looking for a house in his hometown.
4. His twin sister went to the same high school.	**4.** His twin sister is not at the reunion.
5. Armand wore glasses.	**5.** Armand doesn't wear glasses.
6. He was quiet and shy.	**6.** He is talking to everyone and smiling a lot.

1. Armand must work out regularly.

(OR) Armand must have started working out.

2. ______________________________.

(OR) ______________________________.

3. ______________________________.

(OR) ______________________________.

4. ______________________________.

(OR) ______________________________.

5. ______________________________.

(OR) ______________________________.

6. ______________________________.

(OR) ______________________________.

27 Practice

Read Lucinda's schedule for yesterday. Read the conversation and complete the sentences with *can't have* or *couldn't have* and the verbs in parentheses. More than one answer may be possible.

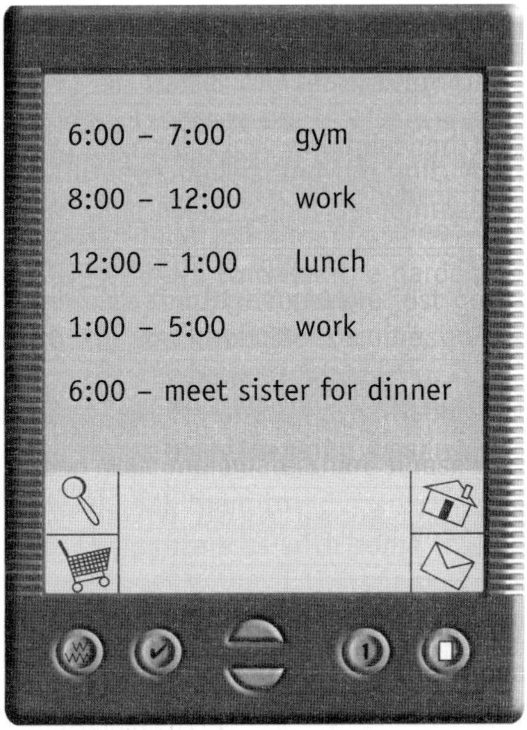

Paulo: Hey, Lucinda! I saw you at the deli yesterday around 11:30.

Lucinda: You (see) <u>can't have seen</u> (1) (OR) <u>couldn't have seen</u> me, Paulo. I was at work.

Paulo: Really? Well, I saw you again outside the bank at 1:30. I waved at you.

Lucinda: That (be) ______________________ (2) me. I was at work then, too. You (wave) ______________________ (3) at me.

Paulo: I did! And you smiled back.

Lucinda: I (smile) ______________________ (4) at you. I wasn't there!

Paulo: That's strange. You even said "hi."

Lucinda: I (say) ______________________ (5) anything. Wait a minute. Was 'I' wearing blue jeans?

Paulo: I think so.

Lucinda: Of course! You must have seen my twin sister, Linda.

7h The Progressive and Perfect Progressive Forms of Modals

Student Book p. 204

28 Practice

Read about Carole, Irene, and Ellen. Then write sentences about Irene and Ellen's schedule for this Tuesday using *should* or *could* in the progressive form.

Carole has two teenage daughters, Irene and Ellen.
Irene and Ellen help around the house.
These are Irene and Ellen's schedules for this Tuesday.

Ellen

Oct 11	S M **T** W T F S
8:00-3:15	study at school
3:45-5:15	do homework
5:15-5:45	straighten the living room
6:00-6:30	cook dinner
6:30	Mom comes home
7:15-7:30	wash (OR) dry & put away dishes
7:30-9:30	free time: watch TV, talk to friends, go online, visit friends

Irene

Oct 11	S M **T** W T F S
8:00-3:15	study at school
3:45-5:15	do homework
5:15-5:45	water the garden
6:00-6:30	cook dinner
6:30	Mom comes home
7:15-7:30	wash (OR) dry & put away dishes
7:30-9:30	free time: watch TV, talk to friends, go online, visit friends

1. It's 4:00, so Irene and Ellen

   should be doing their homework.

2. It's 5:30, so Irene ____________________.
3. From 5:15 to 5:45, Ellen ____________________.
4. At 6:00, Irene ____________________,

   or Ellen ____________________.

5. Then, from 7:15 to 7:30, Irene ____________________.
6. At the same time, Ellen ____________________.

7. From 7:30 to 9:30, they ______________________, ______________________,

______________________, or they ______________________.

29 Practice

It's Saturday. Carole is telling a friend about Irene and Ellen's responsibilities last Tuesday. Write sentences using *should* or *could* in the perfect progressive form.

1. Last Tuesday at 2:45, Irene and Ellen should have been studying at school.
2. At 3:45, they ______________________.
3. At 5:20, Ellen ______________________.
4. At the same time, Irene ______________________.
5. At 6:00, Irene ______________________,

   or Ellen ______________________.
6. At 7:15, Ellen ______________________.
7. At 8:00, they ______________________, ______________________,

   ______________________, or they ______________________.

30 Practice

You are sitting on a bench on the boardwalk at the beach. Complete the sentences with a modal *could, should, may, might,* or *must* in the progressive or perfect progressive form and the verbs in parentheses. More than one possibility is possible.

1. A woman is carrying a surfboard. She (walk) could/may/might be walking to the beach.
2. Her hair is wet, and she's wearing a wetsuit. She (surf) ______________ earlier.
3. She seems tired. She (carry) ______________ her surfboard for a while.
4. She stops. She (look) ______________ for her jeep.
5. There are also two boys running past you. They (race) ______________ to the end of the boardwalk.
6. They are really out of breath! They (run) ______________ all the way from the other end of the boardwalk.
7. The boys are slowing down. They (stop) ______________.
8. They are laughing. They (have) ______________ a great day at the beach!

31 Practice

Read the sentences about teenagers in a car accident. Write *C* if the progressive or perfect progressive form is correct. Write *I* if the progressive or perfect progressive form is incorrect.

_____ **1.** Those kids shouldn't have been standing so close to the highway.

_____ **2.** They could have been waited for a ride.

_____ **3.** Chao and Belinda must not have been hanging out with them.

_____ **4.** We should going to visit them in the hospital.

_____ **5.** They might be waiting for visitors.

_____ **6.** They must not have been paid attention to the cars.

_____ **7.** The police said the traffic light may not have been working correctly.

_____ **8.** They must have been talked loudly. They didn't hear the car coming.

_____ **9.** The doctor said they should be doing well in a couple of days or so.

32 Practice

Complete the sentences with your own ideas.

1. Instead of watching TV, I should be *helping my dad paint the basement*.

2. Instead of doing homework, I could be ________________________________.

3. I should be ____

instead of writing email.

4. Tonight at 6:30, I might be ________________________________.

5. Instead of going to school, I could be ________________________________.

6. One year after I graduate, I might be ________________________________.

7. Instead of spending money, I should be ________________________________.

SELF-TEST

A Choose the best answer, A, B, C, or D, to complete the sentence. Mark your answer by darkening the oval with the same letter.

1. _______ we meet at the theater? We can go out to eat after the movie.

A. Let's
B. Why don't
C. How about it
D. Let's not

Ⓐ Ⓑ Ⓒ Ⓓ

2. We _______ stop by the ATM before we get to the restaurant.

A. let's
B. why don't
C. how about
D. could

Ⓐ Ⓑ Ⓒ Ⓓ

3. Bill prefers seeing movies on a big screen _______.

A. than rent them
B. to rent them
C. or rent them
D. to renting them

Ⓐ Ⓑ Ⓒ Ⓓ

4. Our management team _______ keep as many people as possible than let them go.

A. prefers
B. would prefer
C. would rather
D. rather

Ⓐ Ⓑ Ⓒ Ⓓ

5. **A:** Could we park here for just a minute?
B: _______________.

A. Yes, you could
B. No, you couldn't
C. No, you mayn't
D. Yes, you can

Ⓐ Ⓑ Ⓒ Ⓓ

6. _______ not smoking here? I'm allergic to cigarette smoke.

A. Could you
B. Can you
C. Would you mind
D. Would you

Ⓐ Ⓑ Ⓒ Ⓓ

7. Luckily, no one was home when the tree fell on the house. Someone _______ hurt.

A. could have been
B. should have been
C. may have been
D. must have been

Ⓐ Ⓑ Ⓒ Ⓓ

8. Toru _______ have paid for dinner. He left his wallet at home!

A. shouldn't
B. can't
C. may not
D. could

Ⓐ Ⓑ Ⓒ Ⓓ

9. _______ I borrow your car? I'll be very careful, I promise.

A. Would
B. Will
C. Shall
D. Could

Ⓐ Ⓑ Ⓒ Ⓓ

10. _______ he'll get the computer to work before we leave.

A. Maybe
B. May be
C. Might be
D. Would be

Ⓐ Ⓑ Ⓒ Ⓓ

B Find the underlined word or phrase, A, B, C, or D, that is incorrect. Mark your answer by darkening the oval with the same letter.

1. Buddy would rather (A) stay (B) inside than (C) playing (D) outside with other children.

Ⓐ Ⓑ Ⓒ Ⓓ

2. Suzie would rather (A) having (B) more time off to (C) working (D) a lot.

Ⓐ Ⓑ Ⓒ Ⓓ

3. My grandson maybe (A) sleeping, or he could (B) be playing music. He should (C) be thinking (D) about his future!

Ⓐ Ⓑ Ⓒ Ⓓ

4. We could (A) go (B) to a spa, or what about (C) take (D) a bike trip through wine country?

Ⓐ Ⓑ Ⓒ Ⓓ

5. It's five? They should be (A) arrived (B) by now. We could have (C) given (D) them a ride, but they wanted to walk.

Ⓐ Ⓑ Ⓒ Ⓓ

6. You can (A) have seen (B) me at the carnival yesterday! I was working at home. Maybe (C) you saw (D) me the day before.

Ⓐ Ⓑ Ⓒ Ⓓ

7. I don't know what's wrong. Maybe (A) he fainted. He could be (B) had (C) a heart attack. The ambulance should be arriving (D) soon.

Ⓐ Ⓑ Ⓒ Ⓓ

8. She would prefer (A) have (B) the gold one to (C) the silver one (D).

Ⓐ Ⓑ Ⓒ Ⓓ

9. You should (A) of (B) come! Everyone was there. I could have (C) picked (D) you up.

Ⓐ Ⓑ Ⓒ Ⓓ

10. Jeanine must have been (A) sleeping (B) when I called. She prefers (C) sleep (D) late on Saturdays.

Ⓐ Ⓑ Ⓒ Ⓓ